PRAISE FOR
EXQUISITE MIND

"While Terry's description of how the 'inside-out' understanding has transformed her life is a remarkable story, this is ultimately a book about you. If you let them, the Principles shared in this book will awaken something inside of you — a kernel of hope and possibility that not only can today be better than yesterday, it was designed to be. May your life be touched and transformed as you read this beautiful book, and may you in turn touch and transform the lives of everyone you meet."

Michael Neill,
bestselling Author of *The Inside-Out Revolution*
and *The Space Within*

"Terry's book is the first one of its kind bringing the understanding of innate health and resilience into the world of psychiatry. To give hope and hold hope for people with mental disorders, healthcare professionals will need to fully embrace the concept of personal recovery. The 'inside-out' paradigm of understanding mental distress depicted in these pages leads to a deeper understanding of how our mind works and how true mental healing happens from within us. The author's perspective as a person with lived experience makes it a must read for anyone experiencing any kind of mental distress and loss of hope. This is an immensely enlightening book for families, friends and professionals supporting someone with a mental disorder."

Dr Rani Bora,
Rehabilitation and Recovery Psychiatrist

"Terry Rubenstein has managed to combine her deep understanding of the human condition with her natural ability to teach. This is a deeply heartfelt, honest and touching exploration of the spiritual nature of life and what it means to be human. If you want to gain a transformational understanding of how the mind works and live your life with more freedom, love, joy and connection, read this book."

Chantal Burns,
bestselling Author of *Instant Motivation:
The surprising truth behind what really drives
top performance.*

"In Exquisite Mind, Terry shows us how to get in touch with who we really are so that we can get on with the best possible version of our life. From darkness to extreme clarity, this book will show you how to deal with your own inner voices on a daily basis and how to live a more meaningful, truthful and fulfilled life. This book is a life-changer."

Sammy Margo,
Author of *The Good Sleep Guide*
and *Good Sleep Guide for Kids*

"In a world where alleviating mental suffering often remains a mystery, even for the professionals in the field, the Three Principles represent a fascinating new paradigm in psychological thinking. And crucially, it has already demonstrated the ability to catalyse recovery and transform lives. An "exquisite" book by an inspirational woman."

Dr Harley Simon,
Chief Medical Officer and Executive Vice President,
multinational pharmaceutical company

"It would seem contradictory for an individual's deeply personal story to be wholly impersonal at the same time. Yet Terry's uplifting account — told with humility, honesty and humour — achieves exactly that. This profoundly human story is bigger than being about one person's experiences; it is a narrative that informs all human experience, shedding light and offering a radically new perspective on how our minds work. For anyone serious about having a more peaceful, more effortless, more graceful experience of life, this book will help you to see why that is possible and how it can occur."

Jack Fallow,
Associate Professor,
University of Brunel Business School;
Founder, Centre for Organisation Effectiveness

"This inspiring and beautifully written book outlines a fascinating approach to dealing with life's challenges. It describes positive ways to organise and interpret one's thoughts in practical and spiritual ways. In so doing, its approach can help make one's life more complete."

> Dr Arthur Rubenstein,
> Professor of Medicine and former Dean and Executive
> Vice President of the University of Pennsylvania;
> former President of the Association of Professors
> of Medicine and the Association of American Physicians.

"Terry Rubenstein's personal story in and of itself is achingly honest, deeply hopeful, truly inspiring, and will move your heart. But Terry's gift to humanity is that she has highlighted the universal nature of her story and its application to each and every one of us. Terry will quietly invite you to realise the presence and gift of your own magnificent spiritual nature."

> Dr Dicken Bettinger,
> Founder, Three Principles Mentoring

"One can see the true measure of a person when they face adversity. In this true story of vulnerability, resilience and triumph, Terry Rubenstein demonstrates an inner strength that teaches us that even in the darkest moments of despair, we can still choose our mind-set and whether we show up with dignity and humility. Aside from the courage of sharing her experience, which will be an inspiration to others, Terry's book provides a great and easily relatable introduction into the Principles — even to a novice like me."

> Avron Epstein,
> formerly Head of Investec Private Bank, UK

"This book is an awesome, fundamentally accurate, heartfelt description of the Three Principles paradigm clothed in the brutally honest story of Terry's life. There is no misunderstanding in this book. There is no misleading in this book. This book is truth."

> Tzvi Wurther,
> President, Twerski Wellness Institute

"Anyone who has ever felt 'broken' should read this book. Terry is a remarkable individual who has impacted so many lives around her, and I hope this book reaches many more. Above all her story demonstrates the exceptional power we all have to change our own lives even when it seems there is no hope at all."

> Esther Marlow,
> Director, Carmel Clothing

"Terry's account is so compelling because her story has at its heart, spirit and truth; the formless nature of truth and love are discovered here everywhere! Yet, Terry points as well to practical, spiritual principles that help each of us discover truth in our own lives, in our own hearts, in every moment of every day. A brilliant and courageous woman with a brilliant and courageous tale that should be read by all who care about life and living it fearlessly, no matter their current circumstances."

> Ami Chen Mills-Naim,
> Author of *The Spark Inside*
> and *State of Mind in the Classroom*

"Once I started reading this book I was mesmerised by it. I felt inspired by Terry's account of her challenges and how she had decided to share her experiences to inform and help others. I have learnt so much and feel confident and empowered to apply some of the wisdom within the book to my own opportunities and challenges."

> Elliot Weider,
> Founder and CEO, All Round Leadership

"Terry Rubenstein's book is a unique contribution in a fast growing area. It combines her grippingly honest story with her deep and transformational insight. The combination is a powerful compound that is both highly relevant and credible, offering hope and transformation."

> Aaron Turner, PhD,
> Founder and Senior Partner, One Thought
> Consultancy and Practitioner Training Institute

"As a business leader, mental well-being is fundamental to both myself and my employees. As such, Terry and Brian's book is a crucial part of our library. They should be commended for a first class effort in honesty and down-to-earth but inspirational guidance."

> Paul Deacon,
> Founder and Managing Director, Deacon Search

"This personal and honest account showcases the Principles of Innate Health in a way that demonstrates their practical relevance. The careful reader will acquire an invaluable understanding that will greatly benefit their life."

> Rabbi Dr Akiva Tatz,
> Founder and Director, the Jerusalem Medical Ethics Forum;
> Author of Will, Freedom, and Destiny

"This book takes you into the mind and journey of a person who changed the quality of her mental life in the extreme. When you read this book you will feel like you are taking that journey and gaining the understanding that accounted for her change."

Dr George Pransky,
CEO, Pransky & Associates;
Author of *The Relationship Handbook*

"The teachings contained within this book are crucial for anyone wishing to have a richer, deeper experience of life. As inspirational as Terry's story is, its real value lies in showing how transformation is not just possible, but is readily available to us all. I hope that all members of our large team in our offices across the UK and internationally will read this, as I am confident it will significantly impact them in their personal and professional lives."

Jon Werth,
Founder and Managing Director, Life Residential

EXQUISITE MIND

How a new paradigm transformed my life ...
and is sweeping the world

Terry Rubenstein

with
Brian Rubenstein

First edition published in 2016

© Copyright 2016
Terry Rubenstein

The right of Terry Rubenstein to be identified as the author of this work has been asserted by her in accordance with the Copyright, Designs and Patents Act 1998.

Although every effort has been made to ensure the accuracy of the information contained in this book, as of the date of publication, nothing herein should be construed as giving advice. The opinions expressed herein are those of the author and not of MX Publishing.

Paperback ISBN 978-1-78092-954-5
ePub ISBN 978-1-78092-955-2
Mobipocket/Kindle ISBN 978-1-78092-956-9

Published in the UK by MX Publishing
335 Princess Park Manor, Royal Drive,
London, N11 3GX
www.mxpublishing.co.uk
Cover design by www.simontaljaard.com
Typesetting and book design: www.adirpress.com

Contact the author directly by email: exquisitemind@innatehealth.co

Let your mind be still, for the wisdom you seek
is like that butterfly over yonder.
If you try and catch it with your intellect,
it will simply fly away.
On the other hand, if you can still your mind,
some day when you least expect it,
it will land on the palm of your hand.

Sydney Banks

To

Sydney Banks

and the many other extraordinary teachers
— past and present —
who have encouraged us to look within
for the answers

CONTENTS

Foreword: Michael Neill 1

Prologue: Tears of the Soul 3

Part I: Misunderstanding. 7

  1. Falling Over the Edge of Despair 9
    The Great Depression 9
    Best little girl in the world 13
    Obsessive thinking. 28
  2. Emerging Into the Light 35
    When it is dark enough, you can see the stars . . . 35
    Unconditioned mind 39
    Extraordinary potential of the human spirit 46
    A common thread 51

Part II. Understanding. 55

  3. A New Paradigm 57
    Three Principles 59
    Personal and Impersonal 61
    Mind 63
    Thought 68
    Consciousness 72
    Thought and feelings: two sides of the same coin . . 74
    The missing link 77

4. Psychological Freedom 87
    Personality trap. 87
    Making friends with anxiety 89
    Change is always possible 95
    Truth as the antidote to misunderstanding 100
    Transformative insight 105

5. Living Life From the Inside-Out 111
    Innocent effects of our thinking 112
    Separate realities 117
    Searching in the wrong place 123

Part III. Living With Understanding 127

6. Never-Ending Learning 129
    Living life's ups and downs with more grace . . . 129
    Stepping outside our conditioned thinking . . . 134
    A deeper knowing 138
    An open mind keeps on learning 146
    We have everything we need 149
    Lessons in listening and love 153
    Little people make the best teachers 161

7. The Wellness of Illness. 167
    Pushing too hard 167
    Psychological resilience 171
    Chronic pain and peace of mind 174
    An Exquisite Mind. 179

Epilogue: Revolution of Understanding 186

Further Learning Opportunities 188

With Gratitude 192

About the Authors 195

The Innate Health Centre. 196

FOREWORD

What you are about to read is a true story. It is also a story about truth. In some ways, it's the story of one remarkable woman, but in many other ways it is a description of the extraordinary ordinariness of the human experience. We all face immeasurable challenges over the course of our lives; we are all blessed with the extraordinary resource of what the author calls "Exquisite Mind" — the innate psychological health within us and the spiritual source of wisdom, insight and experience.

Terry Rubenstein talks of a Divine intelligence, but this is not a book about religion any more than her talking about jogging makes it a book written only for those who run. You do not need to be a "believer"; you need only be open to the possibility that there is more to life than you may have previously considered to be true.

I first met Terry several years ago, and to describe her as a force of nature is to be kind to nature. While I immediately sensed her commitment to sharing the Three Principles she describes so beautifully in this book, it took me a bit longer to pick up on the incredible depth of personal experience from which she spoke. Reading about her recovery from an eating disorder, depression, chronic anxiety and then a mysterious illness whose diagnosis and treatment spanned two continents, it is all the more remarkable that she is so straightforward in her presentation and almost comically humble about her gifts as a teacher and healer.

But despite reading about Terry's transformation and the many other people who generously share their own stories about how the "inside-out" understanding has transformed their lives, this is ultimately a book about you. If you let them, the principles shared in this book will awaken something inside of you — a kernel of hope and possibility that not only can today be better than yesterday, it was designed to be. We are all doing the best we can to find happiness and mitigate our suffering; the more we understand what is going on behind the scenes of our personal story, the more successfully we can navigate our lives.

At one point in the book, Terry shares a simple quote from her friend and colleague, Rabbi Shaul Rosenblatt: *"Do you know that all your thinking is not real? The only thing that is real is God."*

By the time you finish this book, you will see the truth of this for yourself, but better still, you will see that "God" is not some abstract ideal, but a way of describing the living wisdom at the very heart of our deepest self.

May your life be touched and transformed as you read this beautiful book, and may you in turn touch and transform the lives of everyone you meet.

With all my love,

Michael Neill
Bestselling author of *The Inside-Out Revolution*
and *The Space Within*

PROLOGUE
TEARS OF THE SOUL

April, 2005

I am in the long, narrow galley kitchen of our house, listening to a track of soulful music and preparing dinner for the kids before they get home. A profound feeling of peacefulness washes over me, as if wholesomeness and well-being are coursing through my body. I feel deeply present, profoundly calm.

Suddenly, I have a flashback of a time not long ago; a time when I was so depressed, so hopeless, so engulfed in despair and pain.

I almost drop what I am cooking. I sit down on a kitchen chair and start to sob uncontrollably for what seems like a very long time. "I am sorry, Terry, I am so sorry," I keep repeating to myself, over and over. "I wish I could have helped you but I just didn't know how. I am so sorry."

Weeping on that kitchen chair with all the smells and sounds of the family's dinner bubbling around me, I realise that, throughout my years of depression and difficulties, I hadn't known how to do better. I am thunderstruck by the depth of this insight. I had done my best. Had I known how to help myself more, of course I would have. But I didn't. And so ensued many dark periods of anguish and sadness.

My self-apology is not because I feel guilty or because I have let myself down. I am simply experiencing the deepest empathy with myself. I am crying with and for the Terry who underwent so much suffering.

And yet there is nothing depressing about these tears. The version of Terry I am crying for is no longer here; she is no longer me. I am letting go and saying goodbye. My weeping is coming from such a deep reservoir of healing. They are tears of catharsis, tears of compassion, tears of connection. They are tears of the soul, of my soul.

I would never have imagined I needed to heal in this way — it was so spontaneous and unexpected — but it was exactly what I required. If this healing episode had not occurred, perhaps I would have looked back with regret and said: "I wish I hadn't gone through that", or "it's too hard to talk about". It is because of my spontaneous crying session that I no longer reflect on my life with guilt, pain, trauma, shame, regret or other negative emotions.

Rather, when I consider the tough times, I see them merely as what I needed to go through then. What has happened to me is the journey I needed to take. There's a resolution, an understanding that my challenges were right and fitting. Sitting alone in that kitchen, there was a wondrous moment of catching a glimpse of clarity in the stark light, when I saw everything with perspective and compassion. I saw my part in it all. Everything made sense.

This is the power of the mind to heal. It offered me an unbidden experience so that I could move on. It does this without us needing to try, or even knowing how to do it. Because we don't know how. But that's just what the mind does. I had unknowingly touched a place of higher consciousness. From that time onward, anything seemed possible.

I had entered a space that I now know is the origin of infinite possibilities, of pure potential. It exists before we construct our 'barrier thinking', thinking that tells us who we are and what we can and cannot do. We unwittingly use this thinking to box ourselves in and close ourselves off. But this universal place of higher consciousness blows the lid off our boxes. It allows us to be so much more than our made-up personalities and limiting beliefs.

That day in the kitchen was testament to how the mind can elevate us if we let it do what needs to be done. It was an immense, perfect, exquisite moment.

*   *   *

A short time ago, in my role as Director of the Innate Health Centre in North West London, I underwent training for our organisation's new website. I was thus introduced to the "back-end" of a website for the first time, a learning experience that was staggering for two reasons:

Firstly, I never knew there was such a thing as a front and back-end of a website, nor had I ever considered this was how a website was constructed. The front-/back-end explanation was novel to me, instantly opening up a whole new world of understanding about the operation of this dimension of cyberspace.

Secondly, it was mind-blowing to see what happened each time I accessed the back-end and made changes to the pages appearing on the front-end. I could add new images, blogs, programme listings and really have a lot of fun. And then, when I clicked on the "Update" button, the front-end of the website (which is what people actually see) was magically changed! I realised that the front-end of the website is *always* a reflection of the back-end. Even though the back-end is invisible to the user, it is where everything is actually created and from where all change emanates.

It is the perfect metaphor for what I intend to share in this book.

Most of us, during the course of our lives, try so hard to create change: in our relationships, jobs, finances, circumstances, feelings and our inner selves. And for so many of us, it often feels like a great struggle. Sometimes, it seems as though the harder we try, the more we perpetuate the problem and the feelings we are trying to get away from.

But we are not told that there is a front-end and a back-end to ALL experience of life. What we immerse ourselves in and often grapple with — the full spectrum of our emotional, mental and spiritual lives — comes from a back-end that we have not been educated about. Without knowing there is a back-end, and without knowing how it works, we are bound to be continually frustrated by the lack of results on the front-end.

This awareness is the key to all change and unlocks real psychological freedom.

Over time, I have come to see that my story — and the story of so many others — is about finding out that a back-end exists. And then understanding how that back-end works.

It is now ten years since I first came across this fundamental explanation of the human experience, known as the **Three Principles**. And over the course of the past decade, not only has it transformed my own life, but the lives of thousands of students and clients I have been privileged to teach. Countless others are being affected by this new paradigm as it sweeps the world.

This is my true story. But it is much more than being just about me. It is about an explanation of a perfectly Exquisite Mind that is available to us all.

PART I
MISUNDERSTANDING

"If the only thing people learned was not to be afraid of their experience that alone would change the world."

Sydney Banks

"I do not ask anyone to ignore their past experiences.
This would be denial, and denial is not a healthy state.
Instead, seek a clearer understanding of the past;
realise that the negative feelings and emotions
from past traumatic experiences are no longer true.
They are merely memories,
a collection of old, stale thoughts."

Sydney Banks

1

FALLING OVER THE EDGE OF DESPAIR[1]

THE GREAT DEPRESSION

There was a time when I felt my whole life was about suffering.

Ever since I can remember, I had moments when I was very low. These weren't just blips or bad days. They were very dark moments. And then they would melt away somehow, and the suffering would ease.

I never understood why there were certain times when I struggled and other times I did not; it all seemed quite random. So I came to the conclusion that I had some kind of chemical imbalance or at least a hereditary predisposition to depression. I dreamt up all kinds of theories and reasons why, but in the end it didn't really matter. What mattered

---

[1] NOTE TO READER: Part I recounts key moments in my story. It is not my intention to write a complete memoir filled with copious biographical details. I share only those pivotal recollections and formative events that will enable you to appreciate the fundamental misunderstandings that informed my first 29 years. But stay with me: the insights that overturned those misunderstandings, which led to a completely different experience of life, come later.

was my belief that I could do nothing about it. It was imprinted in my DNA. This was my script. It was who I was.

I had been prone to mild post-partum depression after the birth of the first four boys, so I wasn't surprised when I started to feel low again within a couple of months of my son Daniel's birth. But what soon began to scare me was the depth of these feelings. This period of depression seemed longer and darker than any that had preceded it. The usual bout of Prozac wasn't helping. Isolated and worn out, I could sense the darkness enveloping me, smothering me, suffocating me. And I couldn't see a way out.

My husband Brian did his best to be supportive, but he was out of his depth. So too, it seemed, were the various therapists and psychiatrists whom I sought out, desperate for some relief from my inner pain. They were well-intentioned yet light years away from understanding what was going on inside of me. We reviewed my past and explored parts of my personality together, but the therapy never seemed to precipitate any lasting change. My heart and soul felt locked. And nobody had the right key, or even knew where to look for it — least of all me.

Things went downhill quickly. Most critically, I did not know how to find the capacity to manage the tumultuous feelings welling inside. Running out of energy and fight, I was overwhelmed with feelings of desperation. A volcano was rumbling within. I had no idea what would happen when it finally erupted.

I managed to hang in there for a while longer. Until the onset of what I would later come to think of as the Great Depression...

October, 2003

I watch the psychiatrist's mouth move as his tired eyes flit back and forth between Brian and me. "I know it's hard to be convinced," he intones, "but the good news about depression is that it does, eventually, get better. You must have hope that this will lift; that you will, in time, feel well again."

But I don't believe him. I glance at Brian, who is squeezing my hand and nodding earnestly, desperate to accept any encouragement that the good doctor is offering. The cocktail of anti-depressants and anti-anxiety medications aren't working. But hope is a very powerful drug to which my loving husband is clinging desperately.

But they just don't get it. I can't feel hope. I can't feel anything. Over the last few months, I have become the "walking dead" and there is nothing anyone can do, or say, or put into my body, that is going to help. Maybe depression does lift for some people, but what has that to do with me? The pain is so palpable, so intense, so entrenched, that it seems absurd to assume that it will release its grip on me, that I will get better. It clings to me like a leech, sucking out the lifeblood, impervious to my futile attempts to shake it off.

I sit in resigned compliance while Brian and the doctor discuss "options". There is further talk of new medication and different therapeutic approaches. An almost out of body experience washes over me in the drab consultation room. I feel as if I have been pulled over to the side of the road and am standing passively next to my car while a police officer issues me with a speeding ticket. I nod dutifully, acknowledge my fate and accept my fine. But this vehicle is steering out of control and it doesn't matter how many warnings, tickets, or corrective driving courses I attend.

Terror wraps its tentacles around me. I am experiencing the worst kind of nightmare — awake, aware and unable to escape. This car is going to crash soon, and who knows how much damage will occur when it does?

For all it matters, the earnest doctor and my caring husband could be telling me that I had just won the lottery. I am so desperately low that whatever they are saying is irrelevant. I am sinking fast and nobody and nothing can save me.

So though my eyes remain open, I shut my ears to whatever they are saying. I just want to rest, to sleep, to escape the noise in my head. Left alone inside my mind, I drift towards the dark memories that always accompany me wherever I go...

November, 1984

I am ten years old, the top student in Mrs Baum's class and captain of the netball team in my local junior school. A good pupil, I have never been in trouble and am well-liked by all my teachers. A button on my uniform has fallen off on the playground somewhere. The others, taking my lead, think it's cool. So each girl asks me to cut off one of their buttons. Unthinkingly, I oblige.

We are called to the headmaster's office where I am accused of being the ring-leader. Mr. Ludke, the strict Afrikaans principal, casts his harsh gaze down on us. We are sure we have a caning coming. But it's my lucky day. I guess he knows I'm a good girl, because we are let off with a stern warning and a disapproving shake of his mop of grey hair. Yet the damage has been done. My bubble has burst, the veil lifted, my true identity exposed. Now everyone will know: I am not perfect.

BEST LITTLE GIRL IN THE WORLD

When I was fifteen years old, I read a book which later became a Hollywood movie. *The Best Little Girl in the World* told the true story of Francesca, an exceptionally talented teenage girl living a charmed life. Until the day she was diagnosed with the severe eating disorder of anorexia nervosa. This was not a story about me. But when I read the book for the first time, I knew instantly that it could be.

Growing up in the privileged northern suburbs of Johannesburg, South Africa, I exerted a great deal of effort in the quest to become the best, most exceptional little girl in the world. The daily, unrelenting battle — the yearning to be popular and pretty and perfect — was all-consuming. When I failed to meet my own impossible expectations, confusion and despair descended.

I needed help to re-align myself to a place of resilience and well-being. But no one and nothing was pointing me in that direction and I lacked the insight to access it from within. In its stead, I was filled with immense anxiety that I would mess up, fall short, let myself and everyone else down. Doubts plagued me incessantly. I would get an A when only an A+ would do. So I just worked harder. But l was chasing shadows. Little did I know that I was looking in the wrong place for fulfilment and meaning. Devastating feelings of disappointment and failure always lurked like shady figures, ready to pounce around the next corner.

I would later come to see that there were two Terrys: one was the version forever intertwined with the story I wove, and to which I had been committed for as long as I could remember. But there was another dimension that remained hidden and obscured. It was the part of me that could feel content and pure and innocent and whole. It wasn't long before the gap between the two versions became a huge, unbridgeable gulf. Frustration, guilt and depressive thoughts occupied the intervening chasm.

The doomed dance of my childhood was amplified throughout my teenage years. Desiring perfection, I continued to obsess about being the best. I must have watched Nadia Comaneci's famous *Perfect 10* performance at the 1976 Montreal Olympics one hundred times. I dreamt of being just as flawless as that brilliant, petite gymnast on the balance beam of my own life. But of course I could not be the best at everything, nor perfect at anything. I could not engineer the outcome which I was convinced my script demanded.

I didn't know where to turn for perspective or guidance. My family seldom engaged in deeper, more meaningful conversations. Feelings, emotions and matters of the soul were not up for discussion. My parents were good people who saw it as their unflinching duty to ensure that our day-to-day material needs were taken care of. Although both of them — and especially my mother — were always around, they lacked the wherewithal to have the kind of conversations I craved. They were doing their best, but they could not offer the insight I needed to help steer me through my confused, disturbing thoughts.

Six years younger than myself, my little sister Lara was preoccupied with Barbie dolls and braiding her long brown hair. Meanwhile, Mark, my older brother by almost two years, was going through his own version of "The Best Little Girl/Boy" story. Considering we were two teenagers with limited understanding and even less perspective, it was no surprise we often seemed to end up encouraging each other in our negative cycles of murky thinking.

Without realising it, I had built fictitious and false realities. Sucked into a black hole of despondent thoughts, I was losing myself. Yet for a long while, my healthy side managed to keep pulling me out, in stark contrast to the underlying dysfunction that often felt all-enveloping. This hinted at a natural well-being that undoubtedly existed within. But at the time, fuelled by my own script and the stories I had been telling myself for so long, I failed to recognise my own innate health. And even when I *did* feel well, I did not know how I could access that feeling more frequently.

Desperate to wield control over something, I developed a fixation with dieting and body image. Nobody could interfere with what I did or did not put into my mouth. In my distorted thinking it was a stepping stone towards achieving my goal — to becoming the best little girl in the world. Deception became both my greatest vice and most necessary skill. I became obsessed with the daily challenge of eating as little as possible and hiding my pitiful intake of calories from my parents, doctors and teachers. And I saved my best lies for the therapists who reinforced my beliefs and inadvertently justified my behaviour.

October, 1991

I steal a glimpse at my watch, hoping she won't notice. Another ten minutes to go until we are finished.

"Terry, I want to ask you something," my therapist says. "Why is it so important for you to be thin? Why can't you just settle for being a normal size, like me?"

I stare back at her blankly. She's nice enough — middle aged, slightly overweight, ordinary looking. I keep my face a mask, but it's a struggle to prevent myself from blurting out what I really want to say.

She just doesn't get it. Why would I want to be like her? I want to be pretty and special and different. The last thing I want to be is normal.

But I can't say that. So instead I smile vacuously and politely respond:

"I'm not sure. Can I think about it and get back to you when I see you next week?"

My mother is waiting for me in the driveway when I walk out of the therapist's rooms. As I slam the passenger door shut, I turn to Mom and declare:

"That woman is light years away from understanding me. I'm not going back to see her again."

And I don't.

Different theories were put forward: I was going through all of this, they told me, because of an inherent, immutable personality; I had a predisposition toward a depressive state over which I could exert very little control; I was the product of how my parents had raised me, and what they and society expected. And yet, for all their experience and qualifications, nobody suggested a different way of understanding my thoughts. Considering it was my own thinking that was limiting my entire psychological experience, this omission carried grave consequences.

I wish I could have understood what was happening back then; it would have helped steer me through the murky waters of my dark thoughts. There *were* good moments, but they had been dulled by the intensity of my struggles during the bleak periods. Drawn to drama in the quest to find myself, I mistakenly assumed that the emptiness within should be filled with intensity and heaviness.

Now, a lifetime of insight later, I realise how hopeless it all was. Nothing demonstrated this more that the extreme contrast between my final A-Level results and my body mass. While my grades soared to such an extent that I received a full university scholarship for outstanding academic achievement, my weight plummeted to frightening levels. When the scales began showing dangerously low numbers, a moment of synchronicity spurred my desperate parents to intervene.

Walking along Cape Town's beautiful Clifton Beach, they bumped into a long-haired, tanned lady who introduced herself as Janet, and soon discovered that she lived only a five minute drive from our family home in Johannesburg. Without explanation, the conversation turned to their respective teenage daughters and the unexpected discovery that both girls were struggling with eating disorders. Mom and Dad were struck by the extroverted, unabashedly warm personality of this unconventional woman, who offered to help them address my anorexia.

When they returned to Johannesburg, my parents offered me a stark choice: enter a hospital-based programme to address my anorexia once and for all, or move in with this comparative stranger named Janet who had assured them that she would be able to help me overcome my severe eating disorder. The thought of leaving my parents' home for the first time left me feeling vulnerable and uncertain. But I knew I had no choice. A part of me understood that we had all run out of options. So in spite of my fears, I went along the Janet path...

March, 1993

I am staring up at the high bedroom ceiling in Janet's sprawling house, which, until a few months ago, was occupied by her ex-husband during their separation period. Janet is different from anyone I've ever known. A free spirit who doesn't conform to the conventions of "normal", responsible, adult living, she is not that dissimilar from the teenager that I still am. Janet says what is on her mind. She doesn't hide her feelings, nor try to avoid the fluctuation of her emotions. The divorce she is going through is painful and leaves her vulnerable, messy and impulsive. But she is experiencing it with a heart and soul that is wide open. There is a willingness to explore whatever she is going through, and I find that at once both refreshing and disarming.

My reverie is disturbed by the high-pitched chime of the doorbell. A moment later, I hear voices at the front door. Intrigued, I make my way from my bedroom and down the long passage, with Janet's fifteen-year old daughter Jesse right behind me.

At the doorway, Janet is embracing a dishevelled young woman — she looks only a year or so older than me — and beckoning her into the house.

"Girls, this is Nola," Janet announces. "She's been sleeping rough on the streets and has got into some bad habits with drugs and a few other nasty things. But now she's going to stay with us for a little while. And don't worry, Nola — we'll sort you out. You've come to the right place," Janet declares matter-of-factly.

Jesse and I exchange a quick glance of recognition. This is typical Janet: unpredictable, demonstrative, overflowing with love and goodwill, and always looking to reach out and offer help to someone in need.

While Jesse shows Nola upstairs to the guest bedroom, I consider how different things are from my own parent's home, less than a five minute drive away. There, all is ordered and predictable. Like most people, we all live within the confines of what makes sense to our own families. There is no way my parents would ever let a drug addict they had met on the downtown streets past our front gate, never mind invite her to live with us. To be honest, I'm not so sure it's a great idea either. Yet it is so liberating to witness an alternative way of embracing life.

I don't know how long I'll stay with Janet, Jesse, Nola and whoever else pitches up. But that doesn't really matter. As long as I'm here, I'm seeing the world differently. Which seems to me to be the best form of therapy and support available right now. It is just what the doctor ordered at this stage of my life.

The fact that Janet barely knew me gave me permission to slip back into a natural and easy way of being. Away from the various script-writers who had played such a key part in my journey thus far, I began to relax internally and see the possibilities of a different pathway. I felt freer than I had in a long time.

This feeling intensified when I suddenly dropped out of my fully subsidised three-year university course after exactly one week. My parents were devastated, their hopes for my future crushed. But somehow I sensed that the pressure and weight of expectation would simply be too much for me. To the outside world, a waif-thin university drop-out, living away from home and clearly too clever for her own good, may have seemed pretty close to rock bottom. But I knew differently. As my weight finally began to stabilise, my troubled soul began to do likewise. Janet was sure she could save me. I had my doubts, but loved her for trying.

I was also trying. Although still a teenager, I dreamed of having a baby. I'm not sure why, but the desire to become a mother, even then, was extremely powerful. But that was not going to happen as long as I stayed so painfully thin. The physiological impact of years of pitifully low body-weight played on my deepest fears that my body would not be able to bear children. And though the irrational desire to avoid putting on weight was still alluring, the longing to have a family one day was even more compelling. This deep, maternal instinct, almost inexplicable in an eighteen-year-old girl, helped pave the way for my recovery. My ever-present issues with food lost some of their powerful grip. There was still a long way to go, but the danger of irreparable damage to my body receded as my weight crept up slowly from its perilous levels.

During this fascinating and surreal period of my life, I also discovered a love of Judaism and its spiritual teachings. Janet herself was going through a period of exploring a spiritually-oriented life; an atmosphere of openness and searching permeated her home, making it rich with possibility. All this was vastly different from the conventional, staid environment with which I was familiar. I was born into a traditional Jewish home, but the profundity and depth of my religion had always eluded me. Now, however, living in Janet's house, I was free to seek out the underlying meaning that I greatly desired. The independently-minded, spiritual seeker in me took over, prompting a yearning to connect, to immerse myself in a divine relationship which offered much more than the relatively superficial, materialistic existence of my first eighteen years. A deeper journey of the self and soul was taking hold.

After six months living with Janet, I returned to my parents' home, and life settled down somewhat. I must have been one of the first students to receive a full scholarship to South Africa's top university and then opt to study as a kindergarten teacher. But I loved the pure, sweet innocence of young children and the intimate atmosphere of the small school where I taught every day.

I had also decided to steer clear of the dating scene. Focussing on my spiritual growth, guys had become pretty much a no-go area for me. Until my brother Mark intervened...

July, 1994

The waiter puts our drinks down with a slight chink and turns away. I look across the table at Graeme and wonder what I am doing here. It is the third time this week that we have seen each other since my brother insisted we go out. Mark was convinced that we would have much in common. He believed that we would be drawn to each other not only by our shared spiritual commitment, but also by our mutual history of attachment to a dark, inner world of psychological complexity.

But I know now he is not for me. An insight emerges. For the first time in my life, I realise I might need a different sort of guy. One who will be less enamoured with the places I've been to in my pained mind, and more interested in those parts of me resonating with health and well-being. I'm not sure yet who that will be, but I know for certain it is not Graeme.

Three days later, I pick up the phone on the third ring and recognise my rabbi's warm, welcoming voice straight away. He is one of those rare breed of men, full of sensitivity and a profound understanding of people. I assume he is going to ask me if I can babysit his kids tonight, but instead, after a brief preamble, he gets down to business.

"There's a guy I would like to set you up with — Brian Rubenstein. He's a couple of years older than you. Not the tallest chap around; dark hair, blue eyes, kind of stocky. He has a university degree, but has also been pursuing his religious studies in Jerusalem for the last year or so. He's back here for a couple of weeks on holiday. What do you think?"

I had seen the boy in question a couple of times. A bit on the short side, but cute enough with a natural, easy way about him, or least that was the briefest of impressions I had gained. Hmmm, I think. Maybe it's worth a try. I let out my breath slowly. "OK, I'll go out with him. Thanks, Rabbi."

I hear the doorbell ring. A minute later, Lara, my gangly-limbed thirteen-year-old sister, comes springing down the corridor. "He's here!" she yells. "And he looks a bit like a cross between Tom Cruise and a chipmunk!" (I'm sure he heard that).

Casting a final furtive glance in the mirror, I adjust my green polo-neck sweater and straighten my navy, knee-length skirt one last time. I run my fingers nervously through my long dark hair before turning away. I haven't put on any make-up — it's not my style — but I have a feeling that won't bother him at all. "Good luck," my mother calls hopefully from her bedroom as I head down the passage.

I glance at my watch while he calls for the bill. I can't believe it's been almost three hours already. We've talked and talked yet there seems to be so much more to say to each other. He's smart and sensitive and has an underlying confidence that stops just short of arrogance. Brian laughs easily, if a little loudly, and I find myself laughing with him. He has an endearing, slightly awkward way about him that makes me feel comfortable; different from anyone I've ever dated before. And when we both stand up to leave the hotel coffee shop, I am grateful I haven't worn my high heels. We're not quite back to back, but I'm pretty sure we are the exact same height.

Brian walks me to the front door. "Thanks so much; I had a really nice time," he says self-consciously.

"Me, too," I reply, instantly worried the words came out a little too quickly.

I close the door behind me as calmly as possible. And then I turn and sprint down the passage towards my parents' bedroom, banging my head on the lowered lintel above their doorway as I leap in delight.

"How was it?" Mom asks, though the outcome of the date is writ large on my beaming face.

"Great!" I exclaim, as I flop onto their king-sized bed. "He's a really good guy. And not too complicated, either."

My parents exchange a hopeful glance while I giggle away like a school girl.

It's our fourth date: we've progressed from anonymous coffee shops to the Lion and Rhino Park on the outskirts of Johannesburg. Brian is clearly becoming more comfortable around me. He is wearing dusty white trainers that don't quite match his navy blue suit trousers and white button-down shirt. (He is not a nerd, but this look is a little too close for comfort.) He becomes serious as an enormous creature with two curved horns ambles past.

"I want to tell you why my parents got divorced when I was twelve," he begins. It's sad in parts and there are tears in his eyes at times, but I get the feeling that he's all right with his family history, that he'll be fine. He shares it all with me, his whole background and the secrets he has kept to himself for so long.

And as I listen, I realise that it is safe to share all of me with him as well. He is willing to trust, to open up, to express his love in spite of — or perhaps because of — everything. He talks too much sometimes, but I can't deny it any longer — I am falling for Brian.

Things happened quickly after that. Lion and Rhino Park date number four took place at the end of July; by mid-September, we were engaged. I had just turned 20; Brian was 23. We were virtually kids; we barely knew each other and we had no discernible plan for making a living, or for creating any semblance of a responsible life. Yet our initial chemistry had taken over and propelled us both forward.

Brian was offering me something precious and rare that I had never experienced before. No matter how much of my inner world I shared with him, he just seemed to want to be with me more. It became clear that whether this was the new Terry or the old Terry, it simply didn't matter to him. He was falling in love with Terry — all of me.

This was my first taste of unconditional love, and unbeknown to me at the time, it was to become one of my most powerful life lessons. Brian was not just the right partner for me. He would be the catalyst for a new understanding of who I really was beneath my own perceived flaws and constructs. He understood and loved me in my entirety — with and without my story — and though it would take time, I would eventually come to see and love myself in the same way.

The breakneck speed of my life showed no signs of slowing down: a mere two years after finishing high school, less than eighteen months since my weight had stabilised, and just over five months since meeting Brian, I was preparing to walk down the aisle and accept him as my life partner. And as he slipped the gold wedding band onto my index finger under the traditional wedding canopy, signifying our formal union according to Jewish law, I burst into the widest of smiles.

Now that I was married, the yearning that had helped me overcome my eating disorder took centre stage. I was desperate to have children. After an anxious wait of almost a year, the day arrived when my elation knew no bounds. And as the long summer days merged into weeks and then into months and trimesters, I allowed myself a glimpse of the most glorious, most elusive of dreams: I was going to become a mother.

From the moment our first son Steven was born in the late spring of 1996, I fell head over heels in love. To call him cute in the classical sense may have been a bit of a stretch; according to Brian, Steven's cone-shaped head bore a direct resemblance to Bart Simpson. But his squashed appearance only added to my joy. Motherhood came naturally to me: there was nothing else I wanted to be doing and nowhere else I wanted to be.

Only a few months later I fell pregnant again completely unexpectedly. Since I was still breastfeeding Steven, it never occurred to me that I would or could conceive again so quickly. There was no time to think about it all, as I was fully immersed in learning the ropes of motherhood for baby Number One. And before we knew it, a second Rubenstein boy had entered the world. We named him Jacob after Brian's late father who had died at a tragically young age.

The contrasting moments of my life were not lost on me. Only a few short years earlier, I had been mired in a state of anxiety, convinced that my eating disorder would affect my fertility. Now, just 23 years old, I was the mother of two beautiful boys separated by a mere fifteen months. How blessed I felt.

Meanwhile, I was discovering that my husband had his own journey to travel. At a time when many people might slow down and consolidate their growing family, we were doing the opposite. Driven by Brian's exuberance and desire to make things happen, the high-speed tempo of our life was gathering momentum. Having completed his two-year communal leadership and study programme, Brian now wanted to use his creativity and energy to make a difference. An exciting, sought-after job opportunity had suddenly materialised and it was not even a consideration that I would stand in Brian's way. So just a few short months after Jacob's arrival we were preparing for a new chapter in London, England.

I was excited and pleased for him. Yet I couldn't help but feel that events were overtaking me, and that I had little or no control over their outcome. Without either of us really realising it, I was finding it hard to keep up, establishing a pattern that would set the tone for the next few years of my life.

Before we knew it, we landed in one of the Western world's largest and rainiest cities on a cold, damp February morning. Within weeks, Brian was fully immersed in his highly demanding, poorly paying, but deeply rewarding work. So while my husband thrived, I focussed on bringing up my two young sons in a grey, impersonal metropolis where I had no friends and an almost non-existent support system. It took all my inner resources to keep my head above water.

We entertained often and extensively, our home a magnet for the students and community members with whom Brian was building relationships and teaching. Our young family and evolving home had its own unique brand of warmth, care, openness and dynamism, giving me confidence and pleasure. At the same time however, I often found myself pushed to my limit — and sometimes dangerously beyond. Attached to a personality that always veered towards the extreme, I struggled to find the necessary balance to cope with the lifestyle we had chosen and to meet the high expectations I always placed on myself.

OBSESSIVE THINKING

May, 1999

"Mommy, look at me!" shouts Steven, as he dangles precariously by one arm from the ladder on the jungle gym. Startled out of my musings, I muster a smile. Lifting my eight month pregnant body off the park bench, I grab the bulging nappy bag and make my way over to where he is playing. Little Jacob looks up from the sand-pit nearby before returning happily to his bucket and spade.

We are in the midst of yet another outing to Princes Park, our "local", just a few minutes around the corner from our rented house in Golders Green. It's a typical London day in early spring: shifting clouds and a slight breeze, but just warm enough for the boys to have discarded their jumpers on the bench for the first time since last autumn. The kids are having a great time and despite my fatigue, I want to join in and encourage their fun. Hoisting myself onto the side of the steel frame, I reach upwards and show my nearly three-year-old son how to grab the bar above his head and shimmy his body along the apparatus.

I become aware that I am the only mother on the climbing frame. Glancing backwards, just beyond where Jacob is playing, I see a gaggle of moms chatting casually on the small cluster of benches located near the front of the playground area. They all seem so familiar with each other. And in that moment, a terrible aching loneliness tears at my insides. While the others laugh and gesticulate at their children, an overwhelming sense of alienation envelops me. They appear so relaxed, so comfortable, so at ease — with themselves and each other. Me? As so often seems to be the case, I am on the outside looking in. I sit on the periphery of life, rather than in the midst of it.

The thought hits me so powerfully: I don't fit in here — in this park, with these people, in this world. I am not fully here, not fully present. As I contemplate my painful isolation, my mind drifts...

"Momma," Jacob calls plaintively. "Where spade gone?"

I release my grip on the jungle gym and shuffle over to the sand-pit. Bending down uncomfortably, I kiss his forehead and pull the tiny implement out of the sand.

The old Terry, full of insecurity and low self-esteem, continued to make a guest appearance whenever the opportunity presented itself. I felt as if I was engaged in a constant, unremitting battle to keep the sadder, darker side of her beyond reach. For long periods, I succeeded. But she was always there, hanging around in the shadows, plaguing me, as she had done for so long, with self-doubt and anxiety. There were interludes of therapy and medication to alleviate those times when she became too demanding and overbearing. There were other periods when she drifted so far away that I thought I might never see her again. But that version of Terry was a persistent bedfellow, and always managed to re-connect whenever it seemed as if we were starting to lose touch.

Seemingly unperturbed by my private struggle, the events of my life showed no signs of slowing down. In something of a blur, a new batch of boys arrived. First Josh, born exactly eight days before Steven's third birthday. That made it officially "three under three". We took a short break thereafter, but the combination of our desire for a little girl and our strong faith played its part. Moreover, though there were moments when I was battling to keep it all together, I was still fully committed to having a large family. Filled with our still youthful and compelling idealism, we ploughed ahead. Benjy, with his chubby cheeks and thick brown hair, soon arrived on the scene. And not long afterwards, somewhat unexpectedly, twinkly-eyed Daniel made it five.

But the pace of our lives was catching up with me. I was exhausted much of the time, overwhelmed almost all of the time. It didn't take long before I began to feel trapped by my life and circumstances. I soon recognised it as more than the depression I had struggled with after the previous births. This battle felt longer, tougher and more hopeless than ever before. Everything seemed so precarious, like Humpty Dumpty teetering on the edge of the wall. There were moments when I felt as if I was crawling to safety. There were others when the fear and desperation were so palpable that I sensed I had already fallen over the edge. I continued to hang in there — barely.

September, 2003

The three older boys are sitting patiently at the table waiting for their supper. Six-month old Daniel is screaming in his baby-swing. Benjy is throwing the food off his high-chair tray. I glance at the kitchen clock. 45 minutes until Brian gets home — at the earliest. Stirring the noodles with one hand, I pick up the phone again with the other and hit redial.

"Hendon Practice, can I help you?" chimes the all too familiar voice of the receptionist at our local surgery.

"It's Terry Rubenstein," I say for at least the fifth time that day. "Is Dr Zokora available yet?"

"Mrs Rubenstein, this is an NHS practice. And as I think I've already explained to you, the doctor is unable to return

calls until after 6pm. I've left him your messages and I'm sure he'll get back to you soon."

"OK, thank you," I mumble with embarrassment, and put the phone down. My eyes drift back to the clock: 5:27pm. I can't wait until 6! Don't they know how desperate I am? I need the doctor to radically up the dosage of my Prozac. Or to prescribe something way stronger. I must anaesthetise the pain. Something, anything. I just need help. Fast.

"Mommy, the noodles are boiling over!" Steven calls out from the table. Returning to the stove, I turn down the flame as water runs over the side of the pot, uttering a silent prayer as I do. "Please, God; just help me get to 6 o'clock."

What was missing for me throughout this period of my life was an understanding of the nature of the mind. Without this understanding, we tend to become consumed with, and overly attached to, our thinking. This leads to strong feelings that we feel compelled to act upon.

But it doesn't matter what we are actually thinking about. When we step back from the content of our thinking and the accompanying feelings, we begin to see an opening of potential beyond our current pain. This is the porthole back to a kinder reality.

But that understanding was still a long way away. In the turmoil of my flailing attempts to cope with the circumstances of life, my negative thoughts and feelings were running amok; they were beginning to overwhelm me. Everyone else I knew seemed to be coping. And so was I — in some ways. Most days I functioned OK, yet I couldn't free myself from the insidious and grim sensation clawing away inside. The slide down a slippery slope had begun, and I was unable to grip any branch to break my fall.

And then everything collided at once. Our nanny walked out on us. In the throes of the chronic digestive disorder which affected all my babies, little Daniel screamed constantly. Four other very young boys clamoured unremittingly for my time and attention. Brian, busy and fulfilled at work, seemed unaware of the extent of my plight. The GP wouldn't call me back. Medication wasn't helping. I couldn't find the right therapist. I felt very alone, a continent away from the friends or family to whom I could have turned for help.

The ominous maelstrom of desperate thoughts swirling inside my head frightened and alarmed me. I was 29 years old with five children. What choice did I have but to stagger along? Like a condemned woman waiting for the executioner, powerless to alter my fate, I quietly swallowed my Prozac and tried not to fall too hard or too fast.

February, 2004

I can hear my son's voice but he seems so far away. My eyes are open but I cannot see clearly. Another one of the boys is calling me but I cannot respond. No part of me is able to move. No part of me wants to move. All I feel is pain — the deepest, most searing pain. I can do nothing to relieve it. So I just lie — and wait...

Brian is calling my name. He is here now. But it doesn't help. It can't help. The pain is too great. It ravages like waves of intense contractions. There is nothing I can do, he can do, anyone can do, to stop it. I resisted for as long as I could, but it has finally worn me down. My body is healthy, but my heart and soul feel broken.

My eyes flutter open, then close. A grave-faced, middle-aged man is looking down at me. He has a white coat. It occurs to me that this is a hospital and I am the patient. But patients can be helped, healed. Not me. The pain feels as if it has always been here. It will always be here.

I catch a glimpse of myself in a hospital mirror. I barely recognise the woman staring back. Her usually olive-toned complexion has taken on a disturbing pallor: taut skin stretched across a gaunt face. I notice black lines under once bright green eyes. The face is mine — Terry's. But I'm not sure who that person is anymore.

Brian's face is etched with concern. He looks terrible. I am asked a question by the doctor:

"How do we know you will be OK? How can we be sure you won't do anything to harm yourself?"

I find the strength to ignore the pain for a moment. And to resist giving the answer he wants. So I say something that I never thought I would:

"You don't," I reply petulantly. "I have choices."

And with that, I collapse back onto the stiff hospital bed, back into a mind full of confusion and misunderstanding.

"The fly, trapped in the bottle,
bangs its head against the glass, trying to find a way out.
The one thing it fails to do is to look up.
The Godly soul within us is the force that makes us
look up, beyond the physical world, beyond mere survival."

Former Chief Rabbi, Lord Jonathan Sacks

2

EMERGING INTO THE LIGHT

WHEN IT IS DARK ENOUGH, YOU CAN SEE THE STARS

I had reached my lowest ebb. Yet to my surprise, within days of returning home from my brief time in hospital, something shifted. Although there was no rational reason, I was filled with an underlying sense of peace. I had endured a very traumatic period in my life and there was nothing obvious in my future indicating that things would be different. Yet I *felt* different. My circumstances had not changed, but in the blackness of the night, it had become dark enough to see the stars.

This sense of peace was deeply reassuring. I intuitively grasped that there was a place within me independent of anything that was happening in my life at that moment — psychologically, physically or on any level. Over the next few weeks this feeling gradually faded. But the glimmer of hope that it offered stayed with me. Not in an obvious way, yet it was there, somewhere beneath the surface. It was comforting to know that innately within a person, deeper than the conscious mind, lies a profound feeling of peace. It was something that I would come to realise as a fact only later.

Heavy clouds were hovering over my life, but in the midst of that intense, paralysing bleakness, a flicker of light had come shining through. That glimpse of hope would be critical: the next few months would prove to be an unpredictable roller coaster. There was still much confusion I needed to sift through in the recesses of my mind before those stars would shine brightly — and stay shining.

June, 2004

I stare vacantly at the framed graduation certificates on Dr Roberts' wall. We are here for our regular appointment, a monthly check-up to assess how I'm feeling, how the medication is working, how I'm sleeping, what other options could be explored. It's been over a year since I started on the most recent course of meds. There are brief periods when I feel some improvement, such as the days immediately following my return home from hospital. But overall I don't really feel as if I am getting better. It's been a long time. Too long.

Meanwhile the meds are affecting me in all kinds of strange ways. I feel jittery and forgetful and detached. I definitely can't laugh, but I can't cry either. I don't remember the last time I felt an emotion deeply. Most of the time, I feel very little at all. I am becoming a ghost, invisible, slowly disappearing.

Brian is asking questions again — he is full of them — so I take the opportunity to slip quietly back from where I came. Inside my head, I don't really hear these two men in dark suits and serious tones discussing my life. But try as I might, I can't shut them out entirely, especially when Brian gently squeezes my hand and asks:

"Terry, are you listening? We've got some important decisions to make about your medication."

I chide myself to keep quiet for a moment so I can attend to their conversation, though if I had a rolling pin on hand right now, it would be aimed at my husband's head.

"Well, I think we need to stick with the diazepam to address your anxiety for at least another few months," Dr Roberts declares.

"I know the side effects are quite disturbing and that your body is very sensitive to the drugs, but we should persist. It will help to stabilise your moods and curb your anxious feelings. And if that doesn't work, we can look at returning to the more traditional anti-depressants like fluoxetine or sertraline. We can also continue with the temazepam to help your sleeping, although there is always the option of a mild tranquilizer like buspirone. Of course, as you know, each of these drugs offer different benefits and comes with a range of side effects, so we'll have to continue to monitor everything and experiment a bit to see what works best for you. But don't worry; I'm sure we'll get it right over time."

Don't worry! Is he joking? Never mind that I feel I need a PhD in pharmacology to understand what the psychiatrist is saying. Of course I'm worried! That's the whole reason I'm here, isn't it? I'm anxious and depressed and experiencing sudden mood changes and barely sleeping. It might be the doctor's job to keep me well-informed, but this guy could do with some serious work on his bedside manner.

Knowing that's unlikely, I retreat back inside myself. Alone with my own dark thoughts, a terrifying image appears: a woman is walking down a long, lonely, empty road. That person is me... but not really. She is a shell, an outer wrapping. Very little is left inside. No spark, no soul.

I have glimpsed my future. If I listen to the doctor and Brian and what well-meaning, sensible people are saying, this is who I will become. My life is already about drugs and psychiatrists and side effects and therapists and new courses of trial medication. I'm heading down a path of stronger and more powerful drugs that I might be taking for a long time — maybe for the rest of my life. I am becoming a well medicated chronic depressant.

The doctor glances at his watch and coughs slightly, indicating our time is up. So we head for the door, promising to make an appointment with his secretary for a month's time.

I am quiet all the way home. Brian tries to engage, discuss how I thought the appointment went — anything to get me to come out of my head. But I cannot vanquish the terrifying image of a heavily medicated, emotionally numb Terry from my mind. Is this going to be the narrative of my life?

A radical thought begins to take root. Right there in the very midst of the darkness, I catch a glimpse of the stars again. They are tantalisingly far away, so elusive. But they are bright and beautiful and illuminate my pathway. I can see them now.

As we turn into the driveway and Brian removes the key from the ignition, I grab his arm.

"Wait!" I almost shout. "I need to say something. Don't judge me and don't interrupt. Just listen. OK?"

He nods slowly, too startled to object. I take advantage of the opening.

"Maybe I don't need all of this. Maybe this isn't really helping me. I don't even know anymore what's making me feel so bad: is it the depression and the anxiety, or the sleeping problems and the other side effects? I think it's time to test what happens if I give the meds a break for a

while. I want to see what it feels like without all of these drugs, so I can assess where I'm really at. I'm losing myself, Brian. I need to feel me again. I need to find Terry. And if it doesn't work, I'll give up and hand myself back to the doctors."

There is a moment of stunned silence. The only sound I hear is the thumping of my heart against my chest. Then Brian shifts his body towards me in the car seat. Taking my hand and giving me his most gentle, loving look, Brian says: "Terry, I don't know about that. It's a very big, risky step to stop taking your meds. And I'm sure Dr Roberts won't think it's a good idea."

He pauses for just a moment as a more determined expression crosses his face.

"But I know you, I can see how certain you are about this. I trust you. I trust your clarity and conviction. This is an incredibly courageous call on your part. But if this is the way you think we need to go, if you are so sure this is the pathway for you to get better, let's do it. I'll support you in this decision. I'll always support you. We'll work it out."

UNCONDITIONED MIND

The decision to drop my medication stands out as a pivotal moment in my journey towards health. But this decision was far more significant than going off all the drugs, though that was exactly what I did. For the first time in a long while, I deviated from the route carved out by my doctors, one that looked responsible from the perspective of society and its cultural norms. I had stepped into a different place inside of myself, connecting with what felt true to me. It was a place I would come to call "formless"; a place that was not already known, tried and tested. I had peeked into a lucky dip and discovered a precious treasure, a new way of moving forward.

Intuitively, I was learning to touch a deeper "knowing" that was there to guide me. I found myself drawing on an intelligence which I would later come to understand, trust and deeply respect. I had stumbled onto the unlimited possibilities of the unconditioned mind. It was one of the most important discoveries I would ever make.

I would not have called this an insight at the time, but I know it as such now. You realise it's an insight when a new thought occurs that feels so intrinsically right you can trust it completely and unconditionally. Amplified by the accompanying feelings of lightness, freedom and clarity, I experienced no doubt or uncertainty about coming off my meds. No rational thinking accompanies insight since it originates from a source that transcends the intellect. It comes from the soul.

Within the fertile expanse of the unconditioned mind, insight emerges as a benevolent gift which resonates with a deep truth and certainty.

I would not necessarily advocate such a drastic measure for others struggling with their own mental health issues. It would be presumptuous of me to give advice regarding their medication and choices. The good doctor and Brian's reservations were well-founded and understandable, but I went with what felt right to me at the time. And I am so grateful that I did.

Unlike Dickens' Pip, I didn't have great expectations. I knew I would struggle. I understood that I would experience withdrawal; that in coming off the meds I might suffer increased anxiety, exhaustion and fluctuating moods. With great effort, I managed to purge myself from a reliance on sleeping pills. It felt like a huge victory every time my body fell asleep of its own volition, even for a short while. I cut out the caffeine. I started to eat better. I read uplifting books and listened to inspiring talks. I became increasingly curious about the human experience. I was fascinated that some people seemed to go through life effortlessly, as if it was theirs for the taking. What was it that they knew that was still hidden from me?

It would be wonderful to imagine that I sailed through the next period of my life. But I didn't. Confusion, doubt and fear did not simply fly south for the winter. The following six months were full of ups and downs, and everything in between. There were times when I felt dreadfully low, and almost buckled. Having dispensed with the psychiatrist and his scripts, I was isolated and exposed.

But I had decided to back myself and so I stayed the course. I wanted to give myself a chance to find the healthy me, the Terry underneath the layers of confusion and medicine-induced haze. Who knew what she would look like when she finally surfaced? My intuition was so strong and true I could not ignore it. And as the haze started to lift, I began to feel clearer, less isolated and more connected to life.

Over time, I noticed that it took less of life to satisfy me. It used to feel as if I could drink a river and still be left with an unquenchable thirst. Now, I could be filled by very little. Whether it was being in the car with the kids, chatting with comparative strangers or spending time in nature, I began to encounter a richer yet simpler experience of all aspects of existence. In meeting myself again, I discovered the joy and security of what I would later come to know as the "inside-out nature of life".

I rejoiced in being able to cry and laugh again, and to feel a range of emotions — anger, pain, elation, sadness, serenity. As my soul started to awaken, I knew I was coming back to life. It was still very tough going, but I couldn't deny that I was more hopeful than I'd been in a long time. I was healing, slowly, but there was a lot more work to be done.

And fortunately, a helper was on his way...

November, 2004

Chris slouches in his armchair, his heavy eyelids closed. I can't tell if he is awake or asleep. He has neither spoken, nor looked at me for at least fifteen minutes. I shift uncomfortably on the soft couch reserved for his patients. I've been telling him how exhausted I am; how much I'm struggling day to day; how anxious it all makes me feel. And just as I'm about to give up on him, he swings one long leg over the other, runs a hand through his thinning grey hair, and shuffles forward in his chair. Opening his light blue eyes which sparkle in a way that belies his 60 odd years, he finally speaks:

"Oh, so you're feeling overwhelmed. Well, you've got five young kids, so that makes a lot of sense to me. I can see that."

I want to shoot Chris. He really irritates me sometimes. But I also know, at this precise moment, why I keep coming to this cramped, stuffy Belsize Park consulting room twice a week — not to mention the added difficulty of having to navigate North West London's arcane parking restrictions. He doesn't need to fix me or save me. He doesn't take my intense introspective thinking too seriously. Ironic as it may sound for a person surfacing from depression, I am coming to recognise that this approach may be exactly what I need.

February, 2005

"I feel like such a failure," I sob, burying my face in my hands.

Chris looks at me with those penetrating blue eyes, a quizzical expression on his face. "I don't really get it," he says with a straight face, though I don't believe him.

I stifle another sob and respond with a noticeable tinge of frustration and self-loathing in my voice.

"I know I'm not a good enough mother. And the same goes for me as a wife, never mind everything else I seem to be getting wrong in my life. I know I can do better and I'm not. I'm just letting myself and everyone else down."

Chris continues to stare at me impassively. And in that moment, I realise he really doesn't get it. He just doesn't do guilt. Period. He can't relate to what I am saying because it's simply not in his frame of reference.

Chris is clever enough to see that I have developed an ideal image of who I should be. But in his world, there is no benefit to be gained by pursuing an idealised self. He recognises that inevitably this will lead to a sense of failure. He understands I am twining a noose around my neck, slowly strangling my inner well-being. Yet his lack of concern for my chronic guilt shocks me. It is hard to believe that anyone could be so uninterested in a pattern of behaviour I had painstakingly cultivated for so long.

In the past I would have argued my case, explained how and why guilt serves me. But this time, something different occurs. We sit in silence and a deep feeling of stillness envelops me. Chris's indifference is a catalyst for my own curiosity.

And then I see it. I don't have to do guilt either. It's not useful to me; it's not serving me in any helpful way. I can drop it now, if I really wish. I can finally let go of this whole notion of my ideal self. I can because I have choices.

So I drop the guilt, just like that.

I never did return to guilt as the strategic pathway to reaching my "ideal self". That snake was no longer coiled around me.

My sessions with Chris gave me the space to talk, to filter and to sift through my thinking. And what he did uniquely well was *not to* take my thinking too seriously. My habitual thinking was all about drama and intensity. But that had no impact on him; it failed to register. He would just slouch back in his chair, tilt his head slightly to the side, and continue to listen and speak and listen some more. There was almost a blithe disinterest in what I was sharing. Whatever was going on inside my own fluctuating drama, he remained outwardly and impassively indifferent to it.

The intensity of what was going on inside my mind had always carried considerable weight for me. I was accustomed to attributing great value to my thoughts, transforming them from neutral ideas into highly potent weapons that framed my feelings and the entire quality of my experience.

Now, for the first time, guided by Chris' reactions, I started to question my own constant stream of noise and commentary. He gave a fresh perspective to all my ongoing internal chatter, helping me to see that there were shades of light, not just darkness.

We experience our thinking as real to us. It appears as fact rather than what it is — just transitory thought. We misunderstand its role, attaching too much importance to our thinking, and in so doing, turn it into a force with far too great an influence.

I was reluctant to let go of old thinking. Yet I could now acknowledge it wasn't serving me. As I began to access something deep within, I found I could release powerful and intense feelings that had held me captive for a long time. The "old" me was habitually drawn to bleakness, to the belief that there was something fundamentally wrong with me. But as we spoke about the choices I had, something began to shift. I no longer felt quite as stuck, trapped by circumstances.

Often, it was less about what Chris said in our sessions and more about my listening. I was discovering that, if I listened deeply enough, I could hear the meaning behind the words, something that transcended what was being said. It was as if I had a built-in barometer that lit up every time I heard truth, guiding me towards my own wisdom. As I stepped outside my preconditioned mind, I became far more interested and curious about what I *didn't* know than learning more about what I did know. I was digging up the tangled weeds that stifled my mind, leaving space in the rich, fertile soil for new understanding to germinate.

This "learning state" was not unique to me. We are all designed to constantly learn and evolve. It is a natural state of mind that is available to everyone. And suddenly it had opened up for me.

After two years of twice weekly therapy with Chris, it was time to move on. I was a different person by then, sensing I could see beyond our conversations, delighting in exploring fresh horizons and discovering parts of myself previously beyond my reach. I felt great potential flowing through me. I was beginning to see a future of countless possibilities previously hidden. I was ready... ready to emerge from the darkness for good.

EXTRAORDINARY POTENTIAL OF THE HUMAN SPIRIT

Throughout this challenging rollercoaster period, Brian was extremely supportive. At a time when our marriage could have been placed under incredible strain, we felt closer than ever before, allies in the joint battle to win back my well-being and mental health. But Brian risked all that when he bought me a gym membership — not exactly my idea of a "get well soon" gift! At first I was resentful; I immediately assumed he had an issue with my weight, which had gone up again as a side-effect of the meds — and hadn't yet come down. But I got over my reaction soon enough, and since he dropped me outside the gym most days, I didn't have much choice: the ageing public library right next door was even less appealing!

July, 2005

A new phase in my recovery has begun. While the stationary bicycle and cross-trainer quickly emerged as my go-to apparatus, there is one machine from which I have steadfastly kept my distance. I am terrified to step on to one of the hulking treadmills looming ominously like a menacing monster waiting to chew me up and spit me out onto the linoleum floor. I have never tried running before — at least not if it isn't in the direction of a NEXT Boxing Day sale — and don't intend to start now.

But over the past few years, I have faced immigration and multiple child births. I have trodden the path of isolation, depression and chronic anxiety. So in a sudden moment of clarity, I decide I am not going to be stopped at this stage by a continuously rolling black rubber mat and a couple of oddly shaped handle-bars!

I clamber onto one of the "monsters" and get going, one step after another after another, gradually building up my speed and intensity. Legs pumping, the adrenaline coursing through me, I find myself thinking:

I don't know anything about how to contend with life and how to be in the world. All my techniques and strategies have failed. My depression has brought me to my knees. I am like a new-born baby who needs to learn from scratch. I need a detox — not to clear my system of medication — but to empty my mind of its tangled, intense and overly-attached thinking.

And I am also discovering that I'm really enjoying this running thing. Surprisingly, I'm pretty good at it. Who knows what else might fall into that category if I'm just willing to give it a try?

The treadmill experience was indicative of a new openness and humility now forming the basis of my psychological and spiritual functioning. I had always considered myself humble, but in truth I wasn't. Although shy, I was full of my own ego without even being aware of it. My crowded thoughts focussing on myself had left very little room for humility. This newly discovered humility offered me a surprising glimpse of the infinite pool of resources available to me: the extraordinary potential of the human mind.

Nine months after that decisive first day on the treadmill in the high street gym, Brian bundled me and my pink Asics trainers into the car one crisp January morning and drove us down to Regent's Park Inner Circle. Pointing smugly at the path, he blithely declared: "Come on, let's run!"

So I started to run. And I ran and ran. We lived less than a brisk fifteen minutes from the magnificent Heath, so at every available opportunity, I found myself there, loping along with the Labradors and well-groomed Hampstead ladies under the wizened branches of those splendid oak trees. I felt the endorphins flowing through me and, fuelled by the power of my own mind, I discovered I could run for long periods over almost any terrain and in any conditions. I did not just become fit. I fell in love with running.

When I returned from these uplifting journeys of both body and spirit, Brian would ask me which route I had taken and how far I had run. He would then proceed to interrogate me about how much liquid I had drunk, how undulating the paths were and what the weather had been like. My answers were invariably vague, a direct consequence of my notoriously poor sense of direction and almost comical inability to discern distances. So I would resort to saying:

"Well, I ran from the house and kind of ended up going past the Whittington Hospital, and then landed up in Highgate Village, and sort of got to the top of Parliament Hill somehow. And then I got a bit lost on the way back so I ended up going round the Heath an extra time or so. But I made it back eventually just before the kids got home from school. I think I ran for a couple of hours at least."

Brian would just stare at me with his mouth open and a look of bewilderment on his face, before managing to ask: "Are you serious? Aren't your legs killing you?" Inwardly, he was probably contemplating for the first time in a long while whether we should go back to see the grave-faced psychiatrist. It's important to record here that around the same time as my extensive excursions to Highgate Village and beyond, he was already the veteran of three London marathons. So Brian's incredulity was justified in his mind based on years of experience as a long distance runner.

But here's the thing: when I was out there running, I didn't notice or think about any of these considerations. I knew nothing about running. It didn't matter to me if it was raining or not; it didn't occur to me that I needed to drink every few miles; it was not even in the realm of my consciousness to worry about the undulating nature of the route. I had no preconceived ideas about running. Instead, I relied on my instinct and common sense. As I said — I just ran...

Until I started training with my loving husband, that is. As the so-called expert (let's face it: the competition wasn't that stiff), Brian attempted to school me in the art of running. And as we began running long distances together, an amazing thing happened: I began to notice steep inclines and bad weather. I started to calculate how far I was actually running, and worry about whether my legs would manage the distance. One day I was bounding up Fitzjohn's Avenue leaving Brian for dead in the pounding rain, as if I didn't have a care in the world (that was such a special moment!); the next day I was dry-mouthed and desperate to reach the summit of a steep hill while fretting over my dripping gear and soaking trainers. Where I had once run ten miles and more without hesitation, I now found these long runs playing on my mind and my body.

What changed — other than the addition of a somewhat unwanted training partner? The distances were no different. My capability, physiology and motivation were the same. London's weather definitely hadn't worsened. But when I reflect upon all that I now know concerning the way we construct our internal experience, the answer was obvious: my thinking about running had changed. Just as my Asics trainers strode a path through the streets of London, so too was my thinking leading the way, forming an impression of my moment to moment experience.

Unbeknownst to me, thoughts about running had snuck into my consciousness, creating a new reality around this once quite simple endeavour. What had until then come naturally and spontaneously was now increasingly subject to various considerations and calculations. Some of the sheer joy and sense of freedom that running had given me dissipated. The carefree runner who simply laced up her trainers and hit the road, to return when she felt like, was in danger of being replaced by a more automated, less natural version.

But I was learning to appreciate the source of these limitations. I grasped that Brian's thinking didn't have to be mine. I could have my own thoughts and my own experience of running. Ever since that critical decision to come off my meds, I had learned to trust myself: my common sense, my intuition, my inner wisdom. It was so liberating to find this confidence in my own mind. So with the greatest of respect to my superstar athlete husband, the next time we went for a long run together... I pretty much ignored him! And in so doing, I revelled in the sheer joy and freedom of a new part of myself that had been dormant for so long.

June, 2006

I feel the sweat trickling down my back, my soaking shirt clinging uncomfortably to my skin. My breath comes in short, staggered bursts. My legs are like jelly. My back is aching and my head throbbing. I cannot see the path clearly; I am uncertain which way to go. It is dark overhead but I must press on. I have very little left to give, but I cannot give up now.

And then, just as I wonder how much longer I can keep going, I burst through the thick, encircling canvas of enormous ancient oaks and into the exquisite sunlight. I come to a halt and take in the immense beauty of the moment. Gazing at the magnificent vista before me, I am profoundly moved. I cannot recall feeling more at peace than at this moment, amongst the pristine rolling hills and towering trees of one of London's most glorious places. Hampstead Heath has never looked more beautiful.

The solitude and serenity that surround me touch my soul deeply. I'm tired and lost and sweaty and aching all over — I must have run at least ten miles already — but the feeling of wholeness welling up within is irrepressible. I sit down on the soft grass and turn my face towards the sun, towards the light.

A COMMON THREAD

Life had settled into a fairly stable routine. Daniel had just turned four and was now in kindergarten for much of the day. As a result, I had more time to myself than I could ever remember — in fact, since Steven, our firstborn, had arrived on the scene almost seven years back. This gave me the freedom and mental space to explore whatever felt right for me.

At the same time as I was developing my love affair with pounding the pavements, I was also reading voraciously. I consumed any book I could lay my hands on about recovery from depression, abuse, illness, or any form of loss or personal ordeal. I was fascinated by stories of overcoming adversity, of immense accomplishment in the face of overwhelming odds. I was yearning to understand how people acquired the capacity to transcend their suffering and trying circumstances. My curiosity was that of a thirsty child, not readily sated. I didn't yet have all the answers, but I was greatly interested in those who did.

So while I ran and read, reflected and recovered, I perceived a common thread at work. Not the little things people discovered about themselves nor the individual insights, but something more far-reaching, a level of consciousness that we all share: the universal power of the human spirit.

Each of us has the potential to transcend our limited thinking, to reach a place of being that exists independently of our experience and circumstance.

We are able to elevate ourselves to higher spheres of functioning whatever our background, upbringing, physical limitations, education, financial status, or other external factors. This potential is not unique to any one type of person. It was available to me. And it is available to us all.

November, 2006

Standing in front of our full-length mirror, I adjust my blouse one last time. A second later, Brian comes bursting into our bedroom.

"Come on Te, we're going to be late. The dinner starts in a few minutes and ..."

"Don't I look beautiful?" I interrupt my husband mid-sentence.

Brian looks at me in sheer bewilderment. Not because I do — or don't look beautiful — but because he has never heard me utter those words. They are simply not in the lexicon of the woman he has been married to for twelve years.

"Um, yeah, you look lovely sweetie," he mumbles.

"Thanks. Now come on, stop standing there with that strange expression on your face. Let's get going."

I grab my coat off the dresser stool and glide past my speechless husband. And as I make my way downstairs, I smile to myself. I do feel beautiful. It is deeply gratifying to know that I can say something about myself — to myself — that I have never said before.

I love the new me that is emerging and I know that Brian does too.

I was returning to a place where I had started off as an infant. A place of quiet and wholeness. A place of purity of mind and purity of soul, where I felt vitally alive and deeply connected. And come one morning, I just knew that I was fully healed. The depth of feeling was so profound. I felt at peace. I felt the beauty of the world. I felt healthy, complete and full of gratitude.

And I fell head over heels in love with myself and the universe.

PART II
UNDERSTANDING

"Throughout time, human beings
have experienced insights
that spontaneously and completely changed
their behaviour and their lives,
bringing them happiness
they previously thought impossible."

Sydney Banks

"The intuitive mind is a sacred gift
and the rational mind is a faithful servant.
We have created a society that honours the servant
and has forgotten the gift."

Albert Einstein

3

A NEW PARADIGM[2]

February, 2007

The rabbi isn't your every-day type of rabbi, and the class he is teaching is not one of your typical classes. It's meant to be the fifth in an eight-week series on the subject of Prayer, but things have taken an unexpected twist. Rabbi Shaul Rosenblatt, clean-shaven and youthful looking, with a touch of a Liverpudlian brogue — and who casually tells us to call him "Shaul" — says we are going to do something different tonight. Having returned only that morning from a conference in Milwaukee, he wants to share his reflections based on what he learned.

"I just spent a few days learning about a novel understanding of psychology known as the Three Principles," Shaul tells us. "These principles were brought to light by a man named Sydney Banks, a Scottish-born

---

[2] In Part I, I shared my story as a gateway for understanding what I had been through and begun to learn. Now, Part II enters into the heart of explaining how my transformation occurred and how life is created at its very essence for all human beings. It focuses on the simple but profound principles at the very core of our psychological and spiritual functioning. The orientation is less one of storytelling and more weighted towards learning. My advice is to be patient, pause to reflect and read over certain passages again if you think that might be helpful. Each chapter is designed to build on the previous one, weaving a tapestry that will hopefully emerge fully as you read, absorb and arrive at your own insights.

welder who had a profound spiritual experience in the early 1970s. There was no obvious reason for him to have had this enlightened experience; by his own admission, Sydney Banks was neither a seeker nor a spiritual philosopher. He was an ordinary man who had an extraordinary moment of profound insight."

While Shaul gathers his thoughts, the rest of us wonder where his observations are heading.

"Over time, Sydney Banks spoke and wrote about this new paradigm based on the fundamental Principles of Mind, Consciousness and Thought. When he relocated to Salt Spring Island on the West Coast of North America, Mr Banks began sharing his insights with both those who lived in the local community and others who came from further afield to learn from him. I don't want to sound overly dramatic, but from what I can gather, these teachings were the beginning of a revolutionary approach towards understanding mental, emotional and spiritual well-being."

I listen quietly from the back row — captivated.

"Before long," continues Shaul, "a willing core of committed teachers began to fan out across North America, sharing this original explanation of the human psyche with widely varied audiences. Two of those people were Dr Bill Petit, a respected, highly experienced psychiatrist, and Dr Judy Sedgeman, a lecturer at the University of West Virginia who holds a PhD in psychology. They were the keynote speakers at the conference I just attended."

When Shaul pauses, an avalanche of questions ensues. Many of the attendees are trying to make sense of this unusual approach to psychology with its spiritual underpinning. They don't know what to make of a rabbi talking about well-being and new paradigms in psychology. To some degree, he also doesn't seem entirely sure of his own grasp of the material. Many of his descriptions of what he heard in Milwaukee are tentative, leading to some confusion and disagreement amongst the audience. So while they ask and argue and analyse, I sit silently, contributing nothing to the debate that rages around me.

Suddenly I start to cry. For a brief moment I am surprised by the depth of emotion that overcomes me. But I am not troubled by these tears, for they are tears of joy, tears of recognition. Everything Shaul says resonates. I have no questions, no objections, no alternative views. A startling conviction and clarity comes over me, a feeling so powerful and profound that I cannot halt the flow down my cheeks.

Shaul has put into words what I have already discovered for myself. I finally comprehend how my life has changed so dramatically in a short period of time. I now have a context to understand the transformation I have gone through over the past two years.

It is time to begin learning the language of the Principles.

THREE PRINCIPLES

The first step was to appreciate that there are three fundamental Principles that explain all psychological experience. Here is how I have come to understand them:

> **Mind** refers to the single intelligent life-source that grants all of us existence and the capacity to think.

> **Consciousness** is the gift of awareness, which allows for the recognition and expression of Thought.

Thought **is the manifestation of what occurs to us at a given moment. Through Thought our realities are created.**[3]

The Three Principles constitute a radical paradigm shift regarding the nature of the human experience: where it originates and how it comes into existence. Here are the facts:

We think, we are conscious of our thinking, and there is a universal intelligence behind this capacity to think.

These Principles illuminate how the potential for human beings is so much more than most of us have ever imagined. Our potential comes from a place that is infinite and unlimited. All experience is rooted in this same, universal origin.

And yet, we experience a subjective version of reality that is a reflection of our own minds, creating the illusion that life is happening to us from the "outside-in".

This is a critical misunderstanding, carrying with it significant and potentially life-changing implications.

---

[3] Whenever the terms Mind, Conscious and Thought are used in reference to the Principles, they will be capitalised. This distinguishes between the Principle of Thought, for example, and the continuous thinking that we experience in our minds.

PERSONAL AND IMPERSONAL

Distinguishing between the "personal" and "impersonal" nature of life is something that few of us ever consider. Even less so do we realise the ramifications of this distinction.

We all have a personal, subjective experience of life which is as transient as it is unavoidable. I think of it as akin to a highly personalised version of a compelling movie that has us on the edge of our seats. My viewing of it is mine alone, as are my interpretations of the plot, my response to the cinematography, my interest in the characters, my appreciation of the humour, my reaction to the horror scenes and my understanding of the film's underlying message. Those sitting beside me, be it my partner or my best friend or a complete stranger, will have their own views, thoughts and feelings of the same film.

By contrast, living life with an understanding of its impersonal nature is radically different. It suggests that this vibrant, dynamic world which feels completely authentic is merely my subjective experience of an incredibly gripping film. When the lights come on at the end of the show I am reminded that however real it seemed, it was only a movie, and I was having my own unique experience of it. Yet, on reflection, I know that an entire process exists behind the creation, production and delivery of the film. Without this underlying system, the movie could not be viewed by a wide and varied audience.

The same applies to the entire psychological experience of human beings. There is a system at work behind the scenes. Understanding how this system operates accounts for the difference between watching the movie as though it were real — and knowing that it is not.

The Principles articulate a fundamental explanation of how our minds work. They are the means to understanding an "inside-out" experience of life.

I had spent my entire life naively looking for security in my experiences. And I think many of us do. We want our relationships, our jobs, our families and our circumstances to be worthwhile, to enable us to feel better. However, I've come to appreciate that because our experiences are essentially no more than fluctuations of thought, they can never offer us genuine security.

We think, we feel our thinking, and then that thinking becomes our experience of life at that particular point in time.

Trying to rely on our moment-to-moment thinking to anchor and secure us is like chasing shadows. We can put a great deal of energy into the chase, but its illusory nature will always mean that we aren't getting anywhere. But here's the good news: the Three Principles *are* constant. They are pointing us towards what *is* always predictable and true.

Knowing that there is a pre-existing system in place that is reliable is hugely reassuring. It awakens us to a bigger picture of life, no matter how frightening, thrilling, seductive, violent, depressing, or chaotic the movie we are currently watching. And in that knowing, we will instantly feel anchored, grounded and secure. That is all I needed. That is all any of us need.

MIND

While Shaul spoke about the Three Principles and the audience got stuck on the concepts and the terminology, I intuitively sensed that the language was simply a tool for explaining the workings of all human psychological and spiritual experience. I knew I needed to look beyond the words to their fundamental truth. The "mind" he spoke of was neither my personal mind nor any other individual mind. Nor was it the biological organism we call the brain. He was pointing us in the direction of a Universal Mind.

I knew that there was a divinity, a creative power, an infinite source responsible for all of life. It was something that I had taken for granted for as long as I could remember. I never went to bed worrying about whether the sun would rise the next morning, whether wild animals would remember how to hunt, whether the rivers would stop flowing, whether the flowers would bloom. I knew, of course, that the seasons would come at the right time (with the caveat that this was London after all!); that the earth would continue to spin on its axis; that the natural world would continue to operate according to its own immutable laws. I knew — and had always known — that there was something taking care of all of that, a pure infinite intelligence, which I called God.

What I failed to see was that the same power, the same source of intelligence, was behind the workings of my mind. It explained why I had often felt so insecure: *because I thought it was all up to me*. I assumed that in order to face life and deal with it, I had to figure everything out and exert greater control over all eventualities. This was a huge misunderstanding. Critically, I was wrong in believing I *needed* to know a lot more. We don't have to know more.

Because there is a Universal Mind that *does* know. It is all-intelligent and all-knowing, providing us with wise and creative thought that is perfect for each moment. Just like our bodies, it self-regulates. It is the origin of all Thought.

You may call it common sense or deeper knowledge or wisdom or higher intelligence or whatever you wish. Different languages, cultures, religions and fields of study describe it in different ways. A Harvard Business Review article may refer to it one way; literature in the Mind, Body, Spirit category of Amazon Books another. But they all point in the same direction.

A short time after hearing Shaul's first talk about the Milwaukee conference, Brian and I decided to do something that would either elevate our marriage to another level — or lead to the domestic equivalent of a thermonuclear war. At a stage when I was opening myself to different experiences, we decided to take a major leap into the unknown: we would run the London Marathon together.

April, 2007

Though we have trained for months with focus and determination, I can't help but worry about the niggling hip injury I am carrying. Nonetheless, it's Marathon day, so I have I resolved to put it out of my mind. I want to enjoy the unique experience of running alongside 37,000 strangers around many of London's most famous landmarks, while half a million of the city's inhabitants cheer us on. It is a glorious day and I am inspired by the magical atmosphere and the great sense of togetherness.

And it's a good thing that I am. Because at the eight-mile mark, my injury has just gone from being a minor problem to a full-blown crisis. I have torn the muscle around my hip.

The pain is excruciating. Equally painful is the thought of having to run a further 18.2 miles in complete agony.

"You're going to have to go ahead," I say to Brian, as I limp to the side of the road. "I'll try and walk the rest of the way."

My husband looks back at me blankly. Like me, he has spent months preparing for this race. Dozens of scenarios have no doubt played out in his head about how the marathon will unfold. But I am almost certain none of them include me bailing out on him before we have even run a third of the required distance.

So we just stand in the middle of the road for what seems an eternity, as countless runners covering the eclectic array of London Marathoners stream past. There are fairies and superheroes; grandmothers and blind runners; rhinoceroses and giant Mars Bars. And then there is the two of us: a wife in immense physical pain and a husband completely flummoxed about what to do next. (Saying something like: "Why don't you take a couple of Ibuprofen tablets and let's see how you get on," isn't going to cut it!)

But as I watch the remarkable sight of the Marathon unfolding, I am hit by the same innate wisdom that has guided me through all my natural childbirths. I know that without medical intervention of any form — be it an epidural or drugs or oxygen — the pain of giving birth seems unbearable. It feels as though the body will break and split apart, as if it is not designed to withstand this degree of agony. I have discovered that the only option is to transcend such thinking, a state of mind I accessed during all my labours. I was able to find some other place that superseded physical sensation, a place separate and less defined by pain.

As with childbirth, I realise now at mile eight of the 2007 London Marathon that again I have to tap into a place beyond thinking about the pain. I must acknowledge it and let it go. I've done it before and I know I can once again harness that remarkable, driving, creative energy with its extraordinary healing power. We are all able to access this transformative capacity when we transcend our "normal" understanding of what can be done.

If I try and walk the next eighteen miles it will only take longer and prolong the agony. In the event that it becomes dangerous or potentially harmful to continue, of course I will stop. But I know I can make it to the finish line.

"Let's go," I say to Brian, who is still standing in his trainers and running-vest with a vacant look on his face. And without glancing over my shoulder to check if he is following, I start running again.

Three hours and eighteen miles later, we advance together down the famous finale along The Mall, crossing the finish line in unison.

At the time of the Marathon I had just started learning about the Principles. It was so reassuring to discover that I didn't need to look far to access a direct experience of Mind, that incredible source of energy that pulsates through us. It had been with me — feeding, fuelling and nourishing me throughout five natural childbirths, and now it enabled me to complete the last eighteen miles of a marathon. It is always present — driving and empowering us.

We aren't alone; there is a system in place that operates perfectly on its own. We are constantly tapping into it without even knowing.

Understanding that this energy source is reliable and constant is a huge revelation. Perhaps this is what people mean when they say they have faith. Faith derives from trusting the system, from knowing that beyond your finite mind is something far more expansive, something infinite that is always supporting you.

The nature of this perfect, self-regulating system is always trustworthy, intelligent, creative and loving. As soon as I stopped trying to override the system by taking it upon myself to think through and figure it all out, I was able to let go. And in that letting go, I found myself falling gently into a welcoming space: thoughts so simple were offered to me, thoughts so precise and so perfect for each moment. My parenting felt right for each of my children. My relationships — with my husband, my parents, my siblings, my friends, and myriad casual contacts — all felt harmonious, uncomplicated and generative. I had all that I needed to guide me through the circumstances of my life. Innate within me was a constant wellspring of common sense, clarity and understanding.

For the first time, I saw Thought as a gift of a Universal Mind — not unique to me but shared by us all. It is knowledge that precedes the intellect; an intelligence that we are universally plugged into irrespective of our background, education and circumstances. Mind is the true source of genuine understanding, not the hard drive of information and memory that has been stored in our brains since we were young.

We all have the capacity to think beyond what we've thought before, to think beyond our analytic minds. We don't need to figure everything out or overanalyse. We don't need to probe and search to make sense of all our experience, past and present. I had always driven myself to look for solutions, to introspect, to think and think and then think some more. I simplistically and naively believed that this approach would generate clarity. And when I finally realised its futility, I wondered why I had never noticed it before. My overly analytic mind was only getting in my way.

> **We are all able to reach a part of ourselves that generates Thought not from any rational dimension, but from the deeper, formless, intuitive mind. This opens the gateway to appreciating the origins of and accessibility of fresh insight, which is the key to dissolving habits of thought and behaviour.**

This is a place from where we heal and evolve. It is where we find resolution and gratitude, compassion and love. It is the home of well-being and wisdom. It is what I have come to think of as the Exquisite Mind.

THOUGHT

Thought is a product of Mind, brought to life through Consciousness. This leads to the creation of all images, perceptions, feelings and experiences. It is what allows us to have any and every kind of mental, spiritual, psychological, and emotional experience in the moment. Thus understood, Thought encompasses more than our negative or positive thinking and the constant noise in our heads.

> **The Principle of Thought transcends the continuous thinking that floods our minds at every turn. It creates our entire mental life. Thought is the energy behind the content of our thinking, and not merely the content itself.**

Back when I was recovering from the Great Depression, and soon after I returned from the hospital post-breakdown, I fired myself. I told myself that the old Terry didn't need to show up anymore; she could take a back seat. I became more humble, willing to learn afresh how to do this thing called "life". The clearing out of the old permitted the new to enter and the necessary insights to emerge. I had come to appreciate that there is a natural flow of new thinking that arises from within.

Previously, my entire life had been filled with thoughts about myself which I was convinced were true. I was not thin enough, pretty enough, smart enough, funny enough or confident enough. I had low self-esteem. I was an anxious person. I was prone to depression. I wasn't good in crowds. I could only relate to people with whom I had a deep connection. The list went on and on.

Now that I had acquired a glimpse into the make-up of Thought, I knew right away the implications: just because a thought showed up in my mind did not mean it was true or reliable. I could now be far more discerning with what thinking I chose to follow.

We cannot stop thinking. That would be like trying not to breathe. But in understanding the *nature* of Thought, we naturally begin to loosen our attachment to our thinking. In so doing, we connect by default to a deeper clarity and wisdom.

By seeing thoughts for what they really are — energy moving through our minds — and not facts or truths, we can have a lighter, less intense experience of life.

This explanation of Thought lies at the heart of psychological freedom.

Children are often our best teachers; never more so than in understanding how Thought works. A tantrum transitions into a fit of laughter within minutes. A new experience with new thought occurs to them almost instantly and they become blissfully disinterested in the previous thought of a few moments ago. Children are not judgemental about their experiences. They just move through them effortlessly, devoid of self-recrimination. Have you ever seen a three-year-old feel bad or beat themselves up about throwing a toy or refusing to go to bed? They live their experiences fully and with great presence, but they don't attach meaning to them. They just have them.

Yet we, as adults, tend to lose that capacity as we grow older. We regard our thinking as more than just energy flowing through our minds. We perceive our thoughts as true — because they *feel* true to us. We then hold on, clinging desperately to our thinking as though it were a life jacket in the sea of confusion that threatens to drown us.

It's not always easy to see through the illusion of Thought. Sometimes, without intending to, we get "tricked" into believing the "reality" our thinking creates...

August, 2001

The house is completely packed. A full lift was loaded onto the back of the huge moving van earlier today. There is not a stick of furniture left, save the two mattresses Brian and I are sleeping on, and some makeshift cots for the kids. Tomorrow at noon we leave London. After almost four years of misery, we are finally going home.

I have been unhappy since I arrived in this enormous city. I didn't want to be here. I haven't been able to relate to the people; I hated the weather. I have felt alienated and alone far too long.

Indefatigable in my protestations, I finally brought Brian to his knees. He agreed to leave and go back home.

But now a radical thought jumps out at me. It shocks me like an intruder emerging from the shadows without any warning. In the dark room, I touch my husband's arm.

"I need to tell you something."

"What?" he asks, half asleep already.

"I don't want to leave. I'm happy here."

Brian doesn't reply for a long while. This man had heard me complain about living in London virtually every day for the past four years. No doubt he thinks I have taken leave of my senses.

"You gotta be joking," he finally says.

"No, I'm serious. I hadn't realised it, but I'm actually very settled. The kids are doing well, I've made some friends, and I'm enjoying the nursery school teaching. I've grown to like this place. I really don't want to leave. London has begun to feel like home and I want to stay."

Another long pause. "Uh, it's a bit late for that, don't you think? Our lift is on the ship already. The new tenants are moving in tomorrow morning. And I'm starting a new job next Monday."

And with that, the man who has been happy here, who didn't want to leave, pulls the duvet over his head and drifts off to sleep.

What happened lying on those borrowed mattresses that final night in London?

My thinking about London, which began even before we arrived, embedded itself in my heart and mind. It therefore became my experience of life in London. But as time went on, beneath the noise of dislike and discontent, another experience was unfolding. I was settling down without realising that was occurring. I was changing and evolving — even if my minds' eye didn't see it. That's just how the system works. Life moves us along.

I was frozen in time because of a misunderstanding of the nature of Thought. But as soon as I didn't need to hold on to my negative thinking anymore — because we were leaving — my thinking dissolved and my unhappiness evaporated along with it. Yet I was so caught in the reality created by my thinking that I couldn't see it until it was "too late". (And in case you were wondering, we did leave the next day. Eighteen months later, we were back living in London.)

CONSCIOUSNESS

I also came to understand that thinking is brought to life via what we call Consciousness. We are born with this gift of awareness; it is built into the DNA of the universe. It is not personal to us. Consciousness is what allows and enables our thoughts to be experienced as reality.

Consciousness is the space in which Thought rises and falls. It provides us with a sensory experience of our moment-to-moment reality, adding colour, form and shape to Thought so that it appears three-dimensional. It also makes our thinking compelling and irresistible, creating the potential for an over-attachment to our thoughts.

In the same way as a movie projector throws beams of light onto a screen bringing images to life, so Consciousness is the screen that gives life to Thought.

That is the power of Consciousness. It makes everything seem real. The net result is that we feel as if the energy running through our minds is true.

Consciousness gives us "real time" experience of our thinking, as if it has an independent viable existence. Take fear, for example. Fear doesn't appear to be self-created. We regard it as a justified response or reaction to something existing in the external world. Invariably, we consider ourselves victims of fear or other emotions because we think they emanate from an outside source. But when we understand that feelings are merely a reaction to Thought brought to life through the "special effects" of Consciousness, we are able to relax and let them come and go. This allows thoughts, feelings and perceptions to flow through us without resulting in any unhealthy attachment.

Glimpsing the workings of Mind, Consciousness and Thought creates a completely different understanding of life. From my vantage point, most models of psychology address the actual *content* of a person's thinking, rather than the fundamental *explanation* underlying it. But once you understand the impersonal nature of the system and how it works, then your personal thinking is put into a different perspective.

When you see that Thought is nothing but a formless or metaphysical energy, your relationship to it changes dramatically. And when you change your relationship to your thinking, it reorganises your understanding of all things. This is because our only mechanism to experience life *is* through our thinking.

With that understanding, one's entire life is able to undergo dramatic, profound and lasting change. Mine certainly did.

THOUGHT AND FEELINGS: TWO SIDES OF THE SAME COIN

In the past, I had treated my feelings with the utmost reverence. Fear, anger, envy, anxiety — I assumed these emotions were substantial and significant. Their intensity would scare me, often without my full awareness. To compound matters, I was constantly puzzled by how to deal with them. Should I suppress my feelings, or express them openly? Should I ignore them, or confront my emotions and risk the consequences? I lived in dread that they would eventually suck me into a black hole from which there was no escape. The best I could hope for was that their intense emotional hold would rule me moderately, like some kind of benign dictator. But this perception, I would later realise, was all back to front.

Feelings are our experience of Consciousness bringing Thought to life through our senses.

> **The link between thinking and feeling is inextricable: they are two sides of the same coin, fundamentally inseparable. We are *always* living in the feeling of our thinking. The inside-out paradigm of the Principles shows how we suffer when we see Thought and feeling as separate.**

Your feelings about life and your circumstances are a direct manifestation of what you are thinking at any given moment — even if that thinking is not apparent to you consciously. Feelings are simply a sensory experience: they are energy running through your system. But for the fact that you are having a specific thought, you would not be experiencing a particular feeling.

Understanding the relationship between Thought and feeling allowed me to finally relax into my experiences and let them rise and fall, rather than suppress or judge them. This sometimes manifested in strange ways, such as bouts of extreme anger I experienced after I came out of the Great Depression. They would appear seemingly out of nowhere, without rhyme or reason. I had never considered myself an angry person before and was therefore shocked by my own behaviour.

June, 2007

Thump! I watch the thick cream-like substance splatter against the wall, leaving a trail of broken glass and large white blobs all over the tiled floor.

"What was that?" Brian calls out in a startled voice from the dining room where he is working on his laptop.

A few seconds later he is standing next to me staring incredulously at the mess I have made in the pique of anger. His usually mild-mannered wife, not known for violent outbursts, has just butchered one of the pantry's key condiments. He has no idea what to make of it.

I barely glance at him, instead riveting my attention on the object of my unrestrained anger — the innocuous, formerly intact jar of Hellman's Extra Light Mayonnaise. And without another word, I storm upstairs to our bedroom, slamming a few doors along the way, leaving my bewildered husband to clean up the remnants of my rage.

The good news is that this fit of anger passed quickly. Within a few minutes I had calmed down and moved on from my childlike tantrum. And yet, this episode was strangely healing and cathartic. Like a kid throwing his toys, it actually made me feel better. That doesn't mean I'm defending my behaviour. I am not generally an advocate of throwing items when upset. But what I *am* saying is that it wasn't necessary to turn my antics into a huge deal. It wouldn't have helped to beat myself up about it. Sure, the whole thing is quite embarrassing in hindsight, but I also realised that I was going through a phase in my healing where I needed to let my feelings rise before dissipating. I didn't need to do anything with or about them; I didn't need to judge them. I just needed to leave them be — and for the first time, I was fine with that.

For so long I had suppressed my rage. Though anger had been lurking like a murky well in my chemistry for many years, it always felt safest to keep my strong emotions in check and under wraps. But I was learning not to become overly concerned about expressing myself. As my thoughts shifted, so did my feelings, and in due course the mayonnaise-throwing moments passed. (Which is a good thing, because Hellman's Extra Light leaves a really oily residue that is quite hard to remove from household walls.)

Incidents such as this showed me that accessing wisdom and clarity does not necessarily mean I am completely happy all the time.

We may experience grief and sadness, anger and loss... indeed all kinds of emotions, and *still* experience a spiritual quality of lightness and a sense of our own well-being.

THE MISSING LINK

Sydney Banks perceived a truth that many others had also seen before. But his clear merging of the psychological and spiritual is, to the best of my knowledge, original. He uncovered a fundamental truth about our psychological and spiritual make-up. The Principles he articulated are, to my mind, the missing link in psychology.

My copious reading of the past few years has included countless stories in which individuals who have undergone much suffering manage to overcome their ordeals. They all point towards something remarkable about the human spirit, a common strand that testifies to the extraordinary human capacity to rise above one's travails. Despite vastly differing circumstances and histories, they share a universal thread that runs deeper than the *form* of their experience. It became apparent that this capacity was within me too, but I didn't know what to call it, how to describe it or how to explain it.

When I first heard Shaul speak about the Three Principles, I realised that he — and now I — had stumbled onto something with the potential to be life-changing. It was an explanation of this common thread: what it was, where it lay and why it remains invisible to so many of us. It was the explanation I had been waiting for.

The Jewish tradition teaches that the unborn foetus learns the entire Torah — all spiritual wisdom — in the womb, but then "forgets" it once born. The process of growing and maturing from infant to adult is about re-learning and remembering what was once known and completely clear. All deeper learning is essentially the re-awakening of an understanding that has always existed.

This is how I felt when I came across the Principles. I was hearing something I already knew. Having experienced my own healing, it was inspiring and heartening to realise that I myself had uncovered this understanding before I actually "found" it. When I learnt about Mind, Consciousness and Thought it only served to explain *how* the shift had occurred. The Principles now offered me a vocabulary and a context. They served as a compass pointing towards my true north, so that should I go off track, I could find the path back.

It wasn't hard for Shaul to notice that I had been deeply affected by the talk he gave on the day of his return from Milwaukee. The pool of tears I'd shed and the fact that I was probably the only person in the room who didn't join in the argument raging around him were dead giveaways.

A couple of days later we picked up where he'd left off at the end of the class and spoke further about the picture that was emerging for us both. We agreed that this new paradigm, so simple and yet accessible, could be of great benefit to others. So under the auspices of the fledgling community-based charity Shaul had recently established, we began organising mini-seminars and workshops, eager to provide an explanation of the Principles to whomever expressed an interest.

Shortly after our first seminar, Shaul asked if I'd be interested in teaching the Principles whenever and however such opportunities arose. This was the closest thing I'd had to a job offer since before my marriage. In the past, I would have found reasons to say "no" and suggest he seek immediate guidance in employee recruitment. But no longer. Although I had no formal training, and was still a novice, I responded "sure" straight away. It just felt right and, in my current frame of mind, no other answer was possible.

In order to get me started, Shaul arranged a one-to-one "workshop" with Dr Aaron Turner, regarded as one of the foremost proponents of the Principles. It was a brilliant opportunity — a focussed, extended learning session with a highly respected and experienced teacher and practitioner of the Principles.

Initially, I was drawn to the intuitive, almost intangible quality of the Principles which lay beyond the intellect. But Aaron was able to add another dimension to my education. He showed me that the spiritual and abstract could also be practical and logical. Aaron's razor-sharp intellect was perfectly suited to conveying this understanding in a manner that made rational sense, whether to business people, academics or trained mental health professionals. Like any mathematical formula, he was able to demonstrate how it all added up.

Even though the *experience* of the Principles must necessarily be one of personal insight, the actual *understanding* is logical. Sydney Banks used to refer to it as "psychologic".

As this logic became clear to me, I began to discern how the Principles could be conveyed to any group, irrespective of their spiritual or practical leanings. Studying with Aaron, I realised that the Principles really were for everyone. Central to this understanding is the premise that human beings at their core are psychologically healthy. Hence many choose to call it *Innate Health*. Mind, Consciousness and Thought are the building blocks that explain our psychological functioning. From then onwards, I would always understand and refer to them as the Principles with a capital "P".

I began devouring a series of CDs and DVDs (back in the prehistoric era before downloads and iPods) featuring talks by Sydney Banks and other Principles educators. And as I listened and learned, absorbed and soared, I was struck time and again by the realisation that this was not a new wisdom or a previously unheard-of truth. These insights had occurred to many others over time; the knowledge had always been available. Thinkers, writers, philosophers, scientists, spiritual trailblazers, religious figures and "ordinary" people navigating their way through life had spoken and written about them in different ways.

Yet there was something new and different in the explanation that Syd and other practitioners offered. In three fundamental principles they encapsulate the missing link crucial to understanding the human experience. These principles are simultaneously practical, digestible and clear, thus facilitating independent learning.

The thinkers and teachers I had previously encountered seemed to grapple with the divide — often a yawning chasm — between the insights they arrived at and the ability to affect others. Transmitting their own understanding in a sustainable and accessible manner presupposed a gap between the teacher and the student. By contrast, the Principles place everyone on the same learning curve.

Each of us has the potential to live our lives from a higher level of consciousness. There is no divide between those who know and those who do not. The explanation that the Principles offer is the bridge, making it entirely possible for every individual to have an independent, fresh experience of their own well-being.

The Principles effortlessly unravel the seeming complexity of human behaviour. They provide a simple yet profound explanation that everyone can access. It matters not whether you are a businesswoman or a stay-at-home mother, a psychotherapist or a vicar, a hairdresser or an executive coach. The Principles transcend nationalities and continents, language barriers and education, background and cultural differences. This wisdom is not only for the spiritually minded. It is not the sole domain of the well-educated or those who have experienced psychological suffering. Inmates in prison and addicts in rehab have been equally affected, as have school teachers and doctors, police officers and teenagers, professors and business leaders.

Some of the narratives of transformation are truly remarkable.[4]

"None of my thinking is real"
Eric's story

I lay on the hard bed in the Eating Disorders Unit of St Ann's Hospital in North London. Everyone could see how low I had fallen. I was a 35-year-old man of normal height who weighed less than 40 kilograms. I had been in that ward for almost a year.

The illness had trapped me in its suffocating grip. It was slowly squeezing the life out of my emaciated body. I had a wife and two young children at home, but I had lost the will to carry on. I felt no hope. I felt nothing at all.

Out of nowhere, a middle-aged man with thinning hair and a youthful face materialised one afternoon by my bedside holding a small hardcover book. He introduced himself as Shaul Rosenblatt. Apparently my wife, Anna, had made contact with him via a neighbour who had attended a session on the Three Principles of Innate Health. I had never heard

---

[4] Eric's story and the other first person "narratives of transformation" that appear later are all true accounts based on in-depth interviews (only names and minor details have been changed). The subjects and their experiences are known to the author through her work, either as clients of herself or of colleagues.

of these Three Principles nor of Innate Health, but lying helpless and frail in my hospital bed, I offered him a chair and asked why he had come.

Instead, he gently but directly asked me about myself.

So I found myself telling him how I grew up in a large family in Vienna, the fourth child of six. I lost my mother when I was only eight and my father remarried a few years later. Within a short time a host of severe problems became apparent. My step-mother was constantly fighting with my father. She and her two teenage sons became abusive and violent towards us. We found ourselves living in a constant cycle of domestic drama, threat and conflict. It was dangerous to be in that house but what choice did I have? I was a twelve-year-old boy with nowhere to go and no one to turn to for help.

My teenage years were desperately unhappy. Every day was a horror — of fighting, of mistreatment, of violence. My younger brother suffered the worst of all; by the time he was a teenager, he was flitting in and out of mental institutions on an almost regular basis. Before long, he had become suicidal. I was not far behind.

I told Shaul how I managed to make it through my school years; how I left home to study further and how I married young. We had kids. I took a job teaching. On the surface, all was going OK. But inside, I was desperately insecure. Something was wrong with me but I could not see a way out. I was so filled with my past that it felt entirely present and real. I was convinced that I was so damaged that I could never be normal.

My depression deepened. I soon developed an obsession with losing weight and was diagnosed with an eating disorder. Within a few months, I had lost so many pounds that I was told I would have to admit myself to a psychiatric ward or the doctors would intervene and admit me irrespective of my wishes.

Although a part of me had always wanted to help myself, I did not know how. I became convinced that I had turned myself into an "eating disorder person". It was inside my body, part of who I was.

In the hospital, I could not avoid my problems any longer. Months and months were spent talking in therapy sessions. Initially it was a relief to talk and be heard. But I realised after a while that I was just going round in circles. We discussed how, with professional help, I could learn to cope and live with my eating disorder. I might return to a normal weight but most likely would always battle my illness.

Almost a year later, I was still lying so feeble in the hospital bed. I had given up on life. Everything was totally bleak.

Anna was incredibly loyal and supportive through it all. But she could not solve anything. No one could.

Shaul listened thoughtfully to everything I was telling him. And then he said:

"Do you know that all your thinking is not real? The only thing that is real is God."

Those words changed my life. My whole body reverberated with the impact. It was as if I'd borne a 50 tonne truck on my shoulders, and with that statement, the truck fell off and vanished.

None of my thinking was real. I had spent almost twenty years convincing myself of the opposite. All the effort, all the therapy — to no avail. And then suddenly this unknown person suggests a radically different way of looking at my situation. Shaul was not a doctor or a psychologist, yet I believed him because on hearing his words, something changed dramatically within me.

We talked some more and then Shaul gave me a book written by Sydney Banks. After he left, I opened it and came across this passage:

"Do you actually believe that everyone has mental health within their own being?"

"Yes, that's the way I see it ... and this inner mental health lies deep in your psyche waiting to be uncovered. It lies beyond the mental activity of personal thought. This knowledge I speak of is sometimes called wisdom."

The enduring truth of those words resonated so strongly that I felt more hopeful than I could ever recall. I gained some weight and left the hospital a few weeks later.

I didn't recover in a day. My intense thinking, which previously I believed to be real, didn't simply evaporate. There was more I needed to learn to help detach myself from the powerful hold of my thoughts.

Many ups and downs followed: a return to hospital, fluctuations in weight and in my mental state. But I had the beginnings of understanding. I knew that there was some place I could turn to for an explanation of what was going on inside my mind.

Shaul came to see me many times. And as we talked, I discovered that the Principles did not focus on curing the illness. Once I had grasped this explanation of the nature of Thought, it meant that I was not ill. There was nothing to solve. I was an innately healthy, well human being who had lost his way for a long time. And now I was finding it again.

As my understanding deepened, the "illness" dissipated on its own, like ice melting away. I soon began to see the implications of my learning in all aspects of my life — my behaviour, my marriage, my parenting. I came to a new appreciation of the human experience — and it changed me as a person.

Five years later there are still moments when I revert to my unhelpful thinking. There are days when my eating disorder rears its head briefly and when I feel that I am suffering again. Yet those words that Shaul uttered that bleak day in the hospital will always be with me. *None of your thinking is real.*

Even when I fall or become attached to my old thinking, I now have the understanding to pick myself up. That is the bedrock of my faith. It is all the security I need.

"When psychologists stopped investigating the connection between mind and soul, they lost two of the most important clues to what they sought. They focussed instead on behaviour, leading us away from our true psychological nature, ultimately encouraging us as passive victims of life."

Sydney Banks

4

PSYCHOLOGICAL FREEDOM

PERSONALITY TRAP

Post breakdown, I unexpectedly discovered a new self. I had always assumed that deep psychological change required hard work. So it was a surprise to discover, through my own experience, that this simply wasn't the case.

The identity that I had painstakingly constructed over almost three decades began to disintegrate. A love of myself blossomed in its place. This was a love of the formless, boundless and timeless essence that exists within each one of us. When I fell into this place of pure potential, I immediately understood that love in its purest form is absolutely impersonal. It is not a human construct.

I no longer needed to look outside of myself for anything. It was all inside: security, acceptance, gratitude and unconditional love. Everything became simpler. Every moment — even those which presented as confusion or emotional chaos — were perfect. Every part of life's unfolding plan made sense.

Outwardly, I hadn't changed. I hadn't had that nose job I'd always thought would be in my best interest. I wasn't any prettier or thinner or more articulate — all imperfections

I had assumed needed correction before I could feel good about myself. They became irrelevant, of no consequence. My fallibilities and flaws were now just part of my uniqueness and contributed to the whole.

Inwardly, my character was undergoing a transformation. I shifted from being shy, insecure, volatile, self-critical, stubborn and impulsive (amongst a few slightly better traits) to stable, secure, flexible, confident and loving. It was a 180 degree turn around. I had found another platform, one that was not constrained by the old assumptions and limiting beliefs.

I had always believed that my personality was a fixed and accurate reflection of my essence and potential. How wrong I was. In no time, I had shed my old persona, almost like a second skin.

> **We are all capable of such transformation once we grasp how firmly we have become attached to a set of personal beliefs about ourselves — and how stubbornly we refuse to let go. It is so liberating to discover that the human spirit is boundless, infinite and not limited to who we think we are, no matter how familiar it feels.**

As I became more of my fundamental essence, so I became less of my own "story", a story that had been unwittingly constructed through the power of Thought over the course of nearly three decades. And surprisingly, losing my so-called earlier identity made me feel only more secure. I was now free to be me. The realisation dawned that I had been living inside a cupboard for so many years, not knowing the cupboard was only one space within an enormous mansion.

That mansion contained doors to many rooms. I had never before entertained the notion of opening those doors, assuming they led to places where I did not belong. Except I did belong in those rooms. I had told myself for so long that I was not a high energy person — until I discovered this was simply not true. I was convinced I lacked confidence — until it became apparent this was another fiction. I was certain that, as a confirmed introvert, I did not enjoy socialising — until I found myself having fun in many situations and connecting with all kinds of people. The rooms of the mansion of my mind were opening up, revealing so much more than I had ever imagined. It was exhilarating to explore new dimensions of myself that had previously seemed inaccessible.

MAKING FRIENDS WITH ANXIETY

Not everything changed instantly. Some habits took longer to shift than others, none more so than anxiety. Anxiety and I had a complex, life-long relationship that required untangling.

August, 2007

That choking feeling is there again — I am never rid of it. I'm anxious. But I'm always anxious, so I guess I shouldn't be surprised.

I am on my way to pick up the boys from school. It's only 4 pm. A long, tiring few hours lies ahead. Supper preparations, homework, cleaning up the kitchen, story and bed time — these are just some of the tasks that my anxious thinking is already clinging to with all its might. My thoughts begin to spiral out of control. Tension surges through me as I wonder how I'm going to cope with these exhausting demands for the remainder of the day. It's that familiar sick feeling in the pit of my stomach, rising like bile in my throat.

Pulling up at a traffic light, a strange thought pops into my head. Anxiety is my oldest, most loyal companion. It's been with me my whole life. As a little girl it accompanied me to my speech recital and then joined me during my ballet exams. It was with me at my final high school graduation and has been a frequent guest throughout my years as mother and wife. Anxiety and I have been almost inseparable for as long as I can remember.

It's a bit surreal but I realise that we are friends in a strange kind of way. So imagining my anxiety is sitting next to me in the passenger seat of our people carrier, I turn to it and say: "Well, if you're going to insist on coming along to fetch the kids, then fasten your seatbelt and let's go."

The woman in the Honda in the next lane looks at me as if I've gone crazy. Maybe I have. But this is one of the most important conversations I've ever had with myself. Because my relationship with my oldest companion is about to change forever.

I arrive at the school and wait for the kids to come to the gate. There's a lot of noise — mothers and teachers and children shouting and laughing — but I don't notice the clamour as much as usual. An unusual sensation comes over me: a burden is lifting, the weight easier. I am lighter, freer.

Back home, I already sense my anxiety has lessened. It is still present, but I am less interested in it than ever before. "OK, let's go bath the kids together now," I tell my companion.

I have made a decision: I will not fight it, feel bad about it or judge it. I experience anxiety. End of story. Like an old, familiar friend, it is still right there with me. But it is no longer as loyal and clingy as before. Its life-long grip is loosening.

And I know now, and forever, that there is nothing to worry about. Whatever happens, anxiety and I — we're going to be just fine.

Previously when I'd been anxious, I blamed the external world: perhaps I had too many children or an inadequate support system? Or maybe there was something inherently wrong with me, some kind of chemical imbalance; a genetic pre-disposition to anxiety. But now it occurred to me: *I can get through sensory experiences. I'm strong enough to do that.*

> **Anxiety is nothing more than a sensory experience we go through. That's it. Period. And when you see it from this perspective, it saps out the potency. The mind reaches a dead-end. And because it has nowhere else to go, it settles down.**

Once this became apparent, it allowed me to have an entirely different relationship with anxiety.

Shortly after I started teaching the Principles, an opportunity arose to attend an intimate conference in San Jose, California, hosted by Sydney Banks himself. Most of those present had already been greatly affected by Syd, as he was affectionately known, and his teachings. Subsequently, they were able to help their own clients, patients, students and communities. I was thrilled to meet many of the mental health professionals who were making inroads in this new field.

After three productive days of learning, I was due to head back to Seattle to catch my return flight to London. But Aaron Turner, who had also attended the conference, had a different idea. Seattle was only a one hour drive from the little coastal town of La Conner, where George and Linda Pransky lived. Here, these pioneers of this new paradigm of psychology ran a Three Principles consulting practice.

"Let's make a detour to La Conner and go and meet Linda," suggested Aaron unexpectedly. "She is just starting a three day intensive with a client and I asked her if you could sit in on a couple of sessions in a learning capacity." (An "intensive" involves working very closely with a single client over a period of a few days.)

Linda is one of the leading Principles teachers in the world and I was bowled over with excitement at the tremendous learning opportunity which had just arisen. At the same time, I was absolutely terrified. I was a novice who had been working in this field for only a few short months. Now I would be sitting in on a client session with a venerated Principles practitioner with over thirty years' experience.

But by this time I had learned enough about the nature of Thought not to take my overly active thinking too seriously. I refused to let my anxiety and apprehension deter me from a chance to learn up close with an expert. So I just pushed through, confident that my concerns were merely the adrenaline rush that comes with fearful thinking. It was no more meaningful than that.

October, 2007

Aaron pulls the car to the side of the road and points to a beautifully appointed two-storey house on the main road of this picturesque little town.

"Here we are, welcome to Pransky and Associates," he announces. "Now, whatever you do, don't say anything," he says to me bluntly. "Just keep quiet, stay neutral and listen to what Linda and the client are talking about."

I nod my head in firm agreement. Of course I'm not going to say anything. I'll be as quiet as a mouse.

The client's name is Julia. A mother of three, I soon discover we have much in common. She spends the morning session talking about her anxiety.

"It is always attached to me like an unwanted appendage I cannot shake off," she says. "Wherever I go, whatever I do, I feel anxious."

I listen with deep empathy and familiarity. I know that old friend well and I know just how persistent it can be.

Suddenly, not long before the session is due to end, Linda turns to me and asks: "Terry, what do you think?"

What do I think? I'm not supposed to say anything. Doesn't she know that? But she's asked me so what am I supposed to do? Ignore her? I'll have to deal with Aaron's remonstrations later.

So I start talking about my own experience of anxiety and my own insight. I tell Julia about my conversation with my "companion" in the car not long ago, and how I chose then and there to redefine the parameters of our relationship.

"I was anxious then and I am still anxious to be in this room right here and now," I tell her.

"But I am not going to let that prevent me from being fully present. I'm not prepared to let it affect my well-being. I choose not to show any respect for anxiety anymore. It is just a flow of thought that is playing havoc with my chemistry — but that's it. I don't need to treat such thoughts as anything else. So I guess what I'm saying is: I'm happy to be here, even though I'm feeling a little anxious. And that's cool. I'm good with that."

I take a deep breath and sink back into the comfy armchair. There's a long moment of silence while Julia absorbs what I've just said. I glance over at Linda and see her looking at me keenly, a soft smile spreading across her thoughtful features.

"I think this is a good time to break," she says. "Let's meet again for the afternoon session in two hours."

During the break, Linda finds me by the cappuccino machine in the downstairs lobby of the practice. I'm stirring some sweetener into my cup when she strolls over and casually observes:

"Well, it looks as though Julia really liked what you said. So, where do you think we should go from here, Terry?"

For the rest of the day, Linda brings me into the conversation where appropriate and consults with me throughout the breaks. She gently guides me, willingly sharing her insights. And all the while, my confidence is growing that I have something to offer and something to share.

CHANGE IS ALWAYS POSSIBLE

When I arrived back in London (and once I had sorted out the leftover lunch in the kids' school bags, which Brian and the boys had turned into some kind of bizarre science experiment during my week away), I was more excited than ever to get things going in the UK. I scoured the country, looking for anyone who had an interest in, or even some exposure to, the Principles. And I was aghast to discover that this big "secret" was barely known. But having been deeply affected by the San Jose Conference, I was determined to share what I was learning with as many people as possible.

At home, things were quieter and more settled than they had been for a long time. Each of the boys was thriving and developing at his own pace. Brian had recently completed his MBA and started a new job in the City. After so many years when our expanding family and full-on tempo had been hard to keep pace with, we had reached a different stage.

It was time to begin sharing what I had learned. Without much of a plan or predetermined strategy, people began to connect with me in order to learn about this new paradigm...

"Consciousness does fall and rise"
Tammy's discovery

I had a very typical upbringing within the relatively insular, secure environment of my local community in North London. I married young and began building a family, happy and content. Life was going well — until my third child was diagnosed with mental delay, a diagnosis which later morphed into severe autism. I was devastated. Lacking the psychological capacity to handle the situation, I became increasingly depressed.

Two years later, another son was born and soon afterwards he received the same diagnosis. I now had two children with severe disabilities. This threw our lives and my inner mental state into turmoil. I saw psychiatrists and therapists, trying different medications and therapeutic approaches with no success. I was slipping into a long, dark tunnel from which I could see no escape.

And then my dear mother died suddenly leaving me completely bereft. I was unable to find the necessary psychological and emotional resilience to cope with the huge loss. I distanced myself from both my husband and the loving but helpless support of my family. They were all struggling, each in their own way, but only I was crashing. Soon afterwards, my father passed away. I went plummeting downwards like a stone tossed into a deep well.

Suffering consumed me. I had no energy at all. I could not get out of bed, brush my teeth, eat a meal. I spent 21 hours a day sleeping. My entire life was crumbling. Guilt gnawed at me relentlessly. "Why am I feeling this way? What's wrong with me?" I asked myself repeatedly. A great heaviness that I could neither see nor understand weighed on me constantly. I was sliding inexorably into an abyss.

The psychiatrist recommended a radical course of treatment: hospitalisation and ECT — electro-convulsive therapy. Desperate and willing to try anything, I decided to go for it. But with great synchronicity, on the same day I was due to undergo the ECT, I spoke to a spiritual mentor of mine. She implored me first to see a woman named Terry Rubenstein who practised something called the Three Principles of Innate Health. Terrified of the ECT and possible consequences, I agreed.

A couple of days later, I went to see Terry... and my life changed forever. All that we discussed resonated so strongly, jolting my mind with a far greater transformational shock than the ECT could ever have accomplished. Terry's words — imbued with understanding, love and hope — pierced the layers of my habitual thinking.

I had long been convinced that I was a victim of very challenging circumstances. I just assumed there was nothing to be done about it. But talking to Terry, I discovered a whole new world of understanding. She suggested that I did not have to remain depressed indefinitely: there was a path out of my darkness.

"There is hope," she said, "if you learn to look afresh at your experience. You are innately healthy."

Terry explained my connection to a Universal Mind. I need not believe that my thoughts were true. I need not let them define or control me. I learned that what I thought did not have to determine my psychological experience, my state of mind. That profound insight enabled me to see the connection between thoughts and feelings.

I saw that I did not have to be held prisoner by my thoughts. I could permit my thoughts to come and go. I could lessen the attention I paid them. Whenever a depressive thought occurred, I would ask myself whether it was really true, whether it really justified the power I attached to it. This was the first step in my recovery from a chronic, debilitating, years-long depression. Within a few weeks of my initial exposure to the Principles, a light appeared at the end of the long dark tunnel.

Lying in bed one night, I experienced a remarkable moment of insight and a powerful surge of energy. Not long after, I wrote this poem in an attempt to capture the profundity and joy of that moment.

"The Missing Link"

As I lay in bed one night
Reading in the dimming light
Oblivious that very soon
I'd be dancing in my room
It hit me straight between the eyes
That consciousness does fall and rise
It became so crystal clear
That just as thoughts do appear
When they are left all alone
They depart on their own
I felt so free, in just a wink
I'd discovered the "missing link"
No more searching would I do
There is no need, I now knew
I wanted to share what I had found
But there was no one around
Everyone was fast asleep
As I'd made this giant leap
And as the realization developed
In love and joy I became enveloped
I jumped out of bed at once
And my feet began to dance
I could not get myself to stop
To jump, to skip, to bounce, to hop
So I danced a merry dance
As I acquired a new stance
All the stars and the moon
Joined with me with a special tune
My life has never been the same
Since that night, when I did gain
An understanding so profound
My whole life just turned around.

The journey towards well-being had begun.

I was struck by how simple the Principles were and how effortlessly my new understanding emerged. I started to see how these same Principles could help others who were "suffering": my children, my friends, members of my community. I was overcome with a desire to immerse myself in further learning, to bring others into this beautiful world of understanding.

Nothing has changed in my circumstances — the basic facts of my life remain. My two sons are still disabled; my parents are both gone; my situation remains very challenging. And yet my whole outlook has changed. I am living out of a completely different place, a place of well-being, love, security and confidence. Every moment is full of possibility and potential.

When I lost my temper with my husband recently, I asked him: "When I behave like this, do you not worry that I am going back to my old self?"

"Don't be silly, Tammy," he replied with a smile. "Your worst moments now don't come anywhere near your best moments when you were depressed."

His response made me realise that there really is no going back to my old self of eight years ago. That version of me was based on a misunderstanding which no longer features. Even when I struggle, and like all human beings, I do, the explanation and understanding I have is watertight.

I never did go through with the ECT. But I did have a very different version of shock treatment, via the gift of learning about the Principles. And like a prisoner released after years of captivity, the liberation of my mind completely transformed my life.

TRUTH AS THE ANTIDOTE
TO MISUNDERSTANDING

The momentum for learning about the Principles continued to build. And then, to our great excitement and surprise, Sydney Banks offered to visit London.

Calling, emailing and texting anyone who might be interested, I arranged a small, intimate two-day seminar at the Hendon Hall Hotel, a five minute drive from where we lived. Pictures of the triumphant England football team from the 1966 World Cup adorned the walls — this was where they had stayed en route to winning the tournament. The hotel (not to mention the players) had aged somewhat during the intervening 40 plus years, but the quiet, old-fashioned, no-frills atmosphere was perfectly suited to Syd's gentle and insightful style.

Straight after the seminar, a piece of good fortune landed in my lap. Syd's hosts had booked tickets to take him to the West End production of *The Sound of Music*. When the hosts had to cancel at the last minute, my friend Chana and I tentatively offered to stand in. I was nervous of this responsibility: we would be sharing some of London's famous nightlife with the venerable founder of the Principles. Yet within minutes of settling into the taxi, I relaxed and ended up thoroughly enjoying Syd's company.

During the intermission while we were waiting for our drinks, Syd turned to me and said: "I'm not sure if you're aware, Terry, but I wrote a few books over the years to help disseminate some of my teachings. One was about a gardener and a group of psychologists. Even though it was just a made-up story, it is full of universal truths."

Syd was referring to *The Enlightened Gardener*, a highly original book written in fable style about the Principles. "Of course I know about it," I replied instantly, almost shouting to be heard over the din of the crowd.

We ended up chatting about insights I had derived from his writings, until the incessant gong sent us scurrying back to our seats for the second half of the show. And while we revelled in the uplifting songs of Maria and the Von Trapp family, I couldn't help but reflect on the conversation. I was struck by Syd's assumption that I may not have known of his books, most unlikely for any serious student of the Principles. The simple humility of that endearing exchange left me touched. Here was a man who had experienced many enlightened moments and had changed so many lives, yet Syd was also down-to-earth, charming and gracious. He still retained a child-like curiosity and heartfelt interest in people and the world around him.

One Sunday evening some time later, I picked up a phone message from Syd on the other side of the globe:

"Hi, Terry. I just wanted to see how you are doing? And I wanted to let you know that I will be giving formal recognition to a few select teachers of the Principles, which I have not done before. Would you be interested in coming over to the States to spend some time studying with me and other practitioners in order to receive that accreditation?"

It just wasn't practical for me to accept the offer at the time, given the demands of my family and other matters in London. But I was moved and honoured that Syd had asked.

Sydney Banks died very soon afterwards. His death was a great loss. But it galvanised those who had benefitted from his wisdom to renew their efforts to teach and share the Principles. And I was fortunate to be part of this process in my own small way.

During this time, three very clear understandings stood out:

Firstly, the Three Principles embody truth. Crucially, an awareness of truth clears up the fundamental misunderstandings which are the root cause of human suffering.

Secondly, because truth operates at the most fundamental of levels, this paradigm could help a lot of people — and help them quickly.

Thirdly, we are designed to connect with a wellspring of insight that opens us up to a new perspective. This capacity is inherent and alive within all of us no matter what.

Like riding a bicycle, once you get the hang of it, it feels easy and natural. In my case it didn't require going for a run, doing yoga or walking the dog to locate that innate capacity. I found it arising spontaneously, effortlessly and sometimes when I least expected it...

September, 2009

I am taking a day off to undergo a straight-forward procedure under anaesthetic in the Sunny Garden Hospital. In a strange way, I am looking forward to it. I'll be relieved of all the usual tasks as mother, wife and working woman that fill my waking moments. The day has been blocked out — in my diary, as well as in my mind.

I'm ushered into a small pre-op room in my dressing gown, those strange back-to-front ones that always make me think they'd be better suited in a psych ward. The male nurse is fussing around, filling out reams of paperwork, wrapping that impossible-to-tear paper tag around my wrist and handling all the countless administrative tasks that keep hospital staff busy. He stops suddenly and turns to face me.

"I'm really sorry I'm ignoring you, Mrs Rubenstein. It's just that I have these forms to sort out and all other bits and pieces to get ready. But please don't worry. Everything will be fine and we'll take good care of you."

"No problem at all. You just do what you need to do," I respond.

How sweet of him to fret that he is ignoring me. I am not worried at all but his care and concern is touching.

The anaesthetist shuffles in and starts asking me the usual questions. "Have you had anything to eat or drink in the last eight hours? Do you have any health issues we should be aware of? Have you been under anaesthetic before?"

I've answered these kinds of questions in the past and do so again now, dutifully. Then the doctor shifts gear:

"I hope you're not worried about this procedure, Mrs Rubenstein. It's all pretty run-of-the-mill. You will only be asleep for about 30 minutes at most. But is there anything you'd like to know or ask?" he asks in a gentle, soothing tone.

"No, I'm fine, thank you."

"That's great. But please let me know if there is anything else we can do to make you more comfortable. And don't worry. We'll take good care of you here. You're in safe hands."

Just as a few moments earlier, I am warmed by the sensitivity, kindness and concern shown me. They are "just doing their jobs", but all the same, I am suddenly and unexpectedly overcome by a deep and profound sense of connection with these two comparative strangers.

Leaning gently over me, I hear the anaesthetist's soft voice: "You'll just feel a little prick and then you can start counting down from ten. 10, 9, 8 ..."

When I awake, I am in the recovery room and my two knights in shining armour (more like green scrubs and hospital masks, but you get the picture) are both waiting to check on me. Once again I am moved by their genuine humanity and empathy. Instinctively, my whole being reverberates with a beautiful feeling towards these two strangers whose paths only crossed mine an hour before. I start to cry. My soul is touched.

When I return home, I tell my sons about this experience. I remark it was probably the most powerful sense of peace and love I have known in the last six months. Unashamedly they ask the obvious:

Why did I feel this way towards the nurse and the anaesthetist, two people whose names I don't even know? Why can't I show the same love towards the more obvious targets: the boys themselves; their father; other family and friends? (Or even Stuart the dog, one of them asks cheekily).

They are mature enough to hear my answer.

"My mind became really still. As I was going under and then coming out of the induced sleep, I had nothing to think about and nothing to do. I could just let myself be. And because my mind was so quiet, I touched a deep place of love, which lies beneath what we consider to be our 24/7 productive thinking. This love is unconditional because it is who we are at our essence. The kind doctor and caring nurse happened to be in the room at the moment when my mind was so still and quiet. And so, they became the natural recipients of my love."

The boys just look at me and nod. What more could they say?

The hospital experience reaffirmed my new-found understanding of love. Love is not the personal and limiting emotion I'd once believed. And it was thrilling to see how such an extraordinary feeling was contained within the quiet of my mind.

TRANSFORMATIVE INSIGHT

As I taught, I found myself speaking increasingly from this feeling space. Intangible and often hidden, it is nonetheless known to the heart and soul. I observed how students and clients discovered their own answers from within their own consciousness, re-connecting with their own common sense. This allowed them to have a different perspective on their "problems". I developed great faith in those learning with me: all I needed to do was direct them towards the Principles and they would do the rest. Truth resonates. They would uncover the potential of their own exquisite minds. They would access their own transformative insight.

The interest in what we were teaching continued to pick up speed. And then the idea emerged to hold our very own conference in the UK. This would be the first of its kind anywhere since Sydney Banks had passed away. With the support of Shaul and our very small team, but devoid of any expertise in organising such a mammoth event, I just decided to go for it.

Barely six weeks later, 140 people crammed into an improvised, subterranean lecture hall at our rented offices to attend the first Three Principles Conference. More people than ever had just gathered in one place in the UK to hear about the Principles. And many of them, as we soon discovered, were deeply affected.

"Everything we have is perfect"
Robin's realisation

My relationship with my in-laws had deteriorated markedly, fast becoming a crisis. They were staying with us shortly after the birth of our third child. Pam, my mother-in-law, was making all kinds of demands on Shaun and me. She was constantly criticising, judging and instructing. In her eyes there was no margin for error — only huge areas for improvement.

Stress and tension simmered beneath the surface. I was walking on eggshells in my own house; I couldn't say what I wanted at my own dinner table. And my husband Shaun was simply not handling it right. He should be doing what I thought he should be doing, not what Pam demanded. After all, I am his wife, mother of his three children. He needed to choose. And he needed to choose me.

I became obsessed with how Shaun was handling, or better yet, not handling the situation. And before long, my angry thoughts had turned in on themselves. If he was the right person for me, he would be managing the situation completely differently. I became absolutely convinced I had made a colossal mistake in marrying this man. So I gave him an ultimatum:

"If your mother isn't gone from the house by 9 o'clock tomorrow morning, I will take the baby, call a taxi and go to see a lawyer to get a divorce!" And I wasn't bluffing.

By 8:40 am, she was gone.

Strangely enough, I was disappointed, because my opportunity to split up had passed. Even with Pam gone, Shaun was clearly the wrong guy for me. After seven years, it was time to face reality. This whole marriage thing wasn't going to work.

I spoke to a couple of friends and they gave me some advice: "Look, you've just had a baby. Why don't you let things settle down a little? It's not the right time to make such a big decision."

So I decided to hang in there a bit longer, especially when I realised that Shaun was particularly good with the children, important because we had three kids under the age of five. I would stay in the marriage for their sake, at least until they were older.

Over time, I became increasingly comfortable with this new situation of living with a man who was clearly wrong for me. Shaun, for his part, wanted to stay and make the marriage work. So I settled into this strange kind of arrangement, living with a decent man and an excellent father, just not the husband I wanted.

About two years later, I received a call from a friend informing me of a first-time conference on something called Innate Health. The venue was just a few minutes' drive from our house and I was intrigued to hear what it was all about. Even better, I saw it as an opportunity to spend two days removed from my husband and the kids. *I'm going on a holiday, how fabulous*, I told myself.

I was so eager to get away from my life that I was one of the first people to pitch up. Sitting on a plastic chair waiting for the first session to start was like relaxing on a sun lounger in paradise. Soon I slipped into a quiet, calm space.

Dr Aaron Turner opened the conference, introducing Dr George Pransky as the keynote speaker. Both uttered a statement I will never forget: "A person's thinking creates his or her reality."

It was a bolt of lightning, an epiphany.

"Oh my gosh, my thinking has created my reality," I said to myself. "I have been making this all up. Everything. All of it! None of it is true." I could have a totally new start; it was a clean slate.

I sat through the rest of the morning session reflecting on this revolutionary approach. And then they called for the lunch break.

I walked up the stairs, flicked on my phone and heard the familiar ping of a voice message. I saw that it was Shaun. He was sitting in the café next door to the conference venue, having come to meet me for lunch. My initial reaction was: "He doesn't trust me. He doesn't really believe that I'm here at the conference. He's checking to make sure I haven't run away."

And then I started laughing. I realised I was just making this whole story up. It was so funny because had I heard his message a few hours before, I would have gone crazy. I would have phoned him and screamed. I would have refused to meet him. In my previous twisted thinking, he would have provided me with yet another reason for splitting up.

But then I stopped and thought: *How sweet, how endearing. That's so lovely. He cares about me. He wants to see how I'm doing. He wants to see me.*

It was a moment of such transformative insight, when I saw everything in a whole new light.

I walked into the café — and there he was. He stood up. I looked at him and I just fell in love all over again. Because standing in front of me was the most beautiful, wonderful human being, husband, father and friend. Everything I could possibly wish for was right there in that moment. Everything about him was perfect. Everything we had together was perfect. We sat for an hour and a half together in that nondescript café and it felt as if it was our first date, our wedding day and our honeymoon all rolled into one.

I went from wanting to divorce this man to seeing him as a completely perfect partner. I realised how blessed I was to be married to him. I had allowed an outside event — the situation with my in-laws — to completely overtake my thoughts. I'd been dismally blind to the overwhelming influence my thinking had been having on me. The Principles had opened up a whole new vista of understanding.

Six years on, I still feel the same way about Shaun as I did that day in the café. That is not to say my state of mind is always good, not by a long shot. But what is incredible now is that when I am annoyed at Shaun or start ranting, I understand the source of my feelings. It is just my thinking; nothing more. I realise I have disconnected myself and have dropped into a lower level of consciousness. And Shaun himself knows not to take notice of me in those moments.

That understanding is my comfort blanket, reassuring me that everything will be fine. And everything absolutely is.

"When our thoughts look real, we live in a world of suffering. When they look subjective, we live in a world of choice. When they look arbitrary, we live in a world of possibility. And when we see them as illusory, we wake up inside a world of dreams."

Michael Neill, The Inside-out Revolution

5

LIVING LIFE FROM THE INSIDE-OUT

May, 2010

The woman in the third row, a vibrant, smartly dressed lady named Nina, is becoming increasingly agitated. She wants answers different to the ones I am offering.

"But I don't understand what you are saying," she declares again.

"My sister-in-law really let me down. And not for the first time. I told her that this was meant to be a family holiday for us all — we had discussed it at length. And they had agreed. Then she suddenly tells me they've arranged something else. And now I'm stuck with this booking and two extra units we've already paid for. So I am supposed to just accept it, let her mess me around, as she has done so many times before?"

I glance around the room at the 50-or-so women sitting on the red padded conference chairs attending our two-day seminar. The first Three Principles Conference had succeeded in informing a wider group of people about the existence of the Principles, so we had turned our attention to another challenge: extending the experience for those interested in further learning.

Having decided to experiment with a women's only seminar, we were quickly over-subscribed. Other than gender they share little in common, ranging in age from 22 to 72 and representing a cross section of the community: a small cadre of school teachers, a headmistress, two clinical psychologists, a GP, the head of a local charity and three or four businesswomen. Others are full time mothers juggling child-care responsibilities; a few are at crossroads in their relationships or career choices; there are even a couple of grandmothers in various stages of retirement from mothering, working or both.

Many of the ladies are nodding along with Nina. Not all have difficult sisters-in-law with a propensity for messing up meticulously arranged family holidays but they do have husbands, partners, children, bosses, colleagues, mothers and friends who seem to give them a hard time in one way or another. All have some experience of feeling "victimised" by people and circumstances beyond their control. They are convinced that this is what causes endless frustration, hurt, anger, grief — in fact, a range of emotions.

My role is to offer Nina and the others a different paradigm to frame their experiences. And so, I begin to teach...

INNOCENT EFFECTS OF OUR THINKING

I only have my own understanding, which is not truth; it's just *my* version of truth so I don't want you to cling to it. But I *do* want you to sense the direction in which we are heading. Our "felt" experience of life originates from a different place than I had always assumed. It originates within our own thinking minds. I used to believe it was derived independently of me — from family, friends, work and circumstances — all restricting factors. But now I know that the potential for psychological freedom is much more than I ever imagined.

Why? Because it derives from a place Sydney Banks calls Divine Mind. It is rooted in the most fundamental, spiritual and universal place. This place is not limited: it is infinitely wise. From this perpetual wellspring anything may arise and be created within your own thinking mind.

For most of us it doesn't appear that way. For the first 30 years of my life I also lacked this understanding. The world we are interacting with is vibrant and compelling, whilst the world of Mind, Consciousness and Thought is totally invisible. So it makes sense that we overlook these fundamental elements. Our experience of life seems to be set in stone, unchangeable and immutable. It feels as if the best we can do is to "think positively". Or, to put it another way, to improve our perceptions of ourselves and our lives, we must change or reframe our thinking.

This is a misunderstanding of the nature of human experience. Contrary to popular belief, we do not experience a reality that is independently out there.

Instead, we experience a reality which reflects our own minds in the moment. The Principles of Mind, Consciousness and Thought point us towards the source of our moment-to-moment experience.

Nina is looking at me as if I am an alien from another planet. She has just exploded with frustration and here I am suggesting that the beliefs she has always held about her psyche may be viewed in a completely different light. But that's OK. I am challenging her understanding of the world. We've got three days together and there is no rush, so I press ahead gently.

As always, I am sharing with you something that I have learned myself: the truth of the inside-out nature of life. But don't imagine I've got it down perfectly myself. I still struggle at times to see that my feelings derive from my thinking in the moment and *not* from my circumstances or from other people. I do have moments, many moments, when I forget or lose myself in seeing the world from the outside-in. And boy, do I feel victimised when that happens.

But the fundamental truth I have learned is this: whatever I am feeling is *always* a direct result of what I am thinking at any given moment.

I know that neither the circumstances of my life, nor the people around me, are able to influence how I feel. And yet, they often seem to do exactly that. How is this possible? Ask yourself why it is that when you engage with certain people in your life, you inadvertently find yourself playing the same old record?

I sense that Nina — along with many of the others — have entered into a deeper listening mode. The explanation of how experience works seems to settle the room down.

Let me tell you what I discovered recently from a relationship in my own life. I have a friend — let's call her Miya — who, for many years, seemed to trigger uncomfortable feelings for me. Or at least that's the way I perceived it. Whenever we interacted, I felt as if she was trying to put me down by noting how perfect her life was — in contrast to mine. I knew she was not doing this intentionally. Certainly she is a great mother and wife, as well as a kind, caring, giving person. But every time we spoke, I was left with the same sick feeling in the pit of my stomach. It was as if I was still in high school competing with other girls as to who was prettier, thinner and more popular.

Although Miya and I were good friends, our interactions bothered me. I had a need to maintain an emotional distance. Yet this didn't sit well with me. Why? Because I knew that the feelings I felt in Miya's presence could not come from her or from anyone else for that matter. They could *only* come from Thought. Thought is always the only source.

During this period, I was working with a client who was having a similarly frustrating relationship with a close friend of hers. I shared with her the inside-out nature of experience: how her feelings were *always* the manifestation of her thinking in the moment and how understanding the nature of Thought was the key to creating a different dynamic with her friend.

While I was sharing this perspective with my client, the learning reversed and turned in on me. Miya was someone I was fond of and admired. Yet our relationship seemed to invoke uncomfortable feelings in me. But based on my understanding of the Principles — which I was sharing with my own client — I realised our friendship could take a very different course.

I knew that my experience of the relationship was being formed via my own thinking mind. This was the only possible way for it to form. So I stepped back from my own thinking. Instantly a flood of new thought washed over me. I became filled with understanding, compassion and empathy.

Everything changed after that, at least for me. I felt differently about Miya because *I was thinking differently about her*. No other reason. It's the way it works.

How powerful is that? Miya was probably behaving in the same way and saying the same things. But I was having a different experience of her. Because I had been gifted to see once again that there was nothing limiting my experience but my own misunderstanding of where it was coming from.

I am quiet for a long moment as my words drift over the group and settle. There is a soft, warm, connecting atmosphere in the hall. I hear the gentle whir of the air-conditioning unit but otherwise all is quiet. Nobody asks any questions or offers any comments. I absorb the collective consciousness and my senses come alive. It is moments like this when I love my work so much.

Yes, Nina, it would appear as if your sister-in-law is limiting your capacity for joy and a wonderful vacation. But if you look behind the veil of your perceptions, you will always find it is your thinking which brings your senses to life. Your thinking informs you. It creates your feelings towards your sister-in-law in any given moment. Once you know this, you can cut the umbilical cord of your experience which was mistakenly tied to someone else. It gives you back your freedom, allowing you to see life with a fresh perspective, again and again and again.

I have observed my thinking and feelings for almost a decade and here's what I have come to appreciate: we react unawares to Thought — and then blame others for our reactions:

Thought and feeling show up so quickly and seamlessly that it looks as if we never actually *thought* our reality, but merely participated as innocent bystanders.

If we are willing to look beyond what appears real, we will see the creative intelligence that manifests as Thought creating our moment-to-moment reality in nanoseconds.

I pause again, allowing the group to absorb all that we have been discussing, before gently directing my gaze back towards Nina.

> At the same time, you will continue to realise that you are not a victim of challenging individuals. Instead, you will experience psychological freedom as you begin to discover that Thought is infinite and neutral. The free flow of thinking is endless. There is no limit to how creative it can be.

I look up at the clock on the back wall and notice we are close to our anticipated end time. I don't have anything more to offer right now. And Nina and the rest of the group seem to have absorbed enough for the day.

SEPARATE REALITIES

Towards mid-afternoon on the second day, Sharon, a slightly older woman from South London who had attended a couple of my previous talks, cannot contain herself any longer.

"Terry, I am definitely beginning to see the impact of my own mind on all aspects of my life. But something is still jarring for me. Let me tell you what I have to deal with on an almost daily basis. My eighteen-year-old son won't listen to what either his father or I say to him. He won't help, and completely does his own thing. It sets a bad example for the younger ones. We want him to appreciate that he is part of a family, part of a system. This isn't an unreasonable expectation. But he's just not prepared to play ball. So I'd appreciate some specific advice how to handle my son. It's all good and well to say the issues with him are coming from the inside-out but how is this of any practical help? It's all a bit vague to me."

I understand what Sharon is grappling with. Intellectually she grasps the logic that the frustration with her son is coming from within. But it hasn't landed as a true insight for her. So it doesn't look practical.

> I know you'd like me to offer some prescriptive guidance, Sharon. But I'm going to stick with what we've been talking about. An understanding of the Principles always offers us the pathway. It allows us to step back from our specific situations in order to derive the insight regarding what is really going on — for your son and for yourself. The key issue to consider is this: who is playing the lead role in your relationship? If it is still your son who is dictating the nature of your response, then it's always going to be an outside-in experience. And that will inevitably feel limiting, if not infuriating.

Casting my eyes around the room, I notice that the ladies are engaged and connected. Clearly this conversation strikes a chord, though I sense that a specific example from my own life will help further. But before I have the chance, a familiar voice calls out from the third row.

"I get it!" Nina exclaims. "I've been thinking it over since our discussion yesterday morning. For all this time I've been holding onto resentment towards my sister-in-law because she messed up our holiday plans — or at least that was my perception. But I see now that I gain nothing from holding on to these thoughts. I just end up suffering the feelings that come with them. It's pointless. I'm clinging to a misunderstanding that is not serving me at all. I had assumed my reaction was appropriate and justified, but that's ridiculous! It will be fascinating to see what emerges for me now that my resentment no longer makes any sense."

Nina is seated on the edge of her chair, an animated grin spread across her face. I am used to "pop-up" teachers appearing unannounced in my classes. Inspired by their own insight, they can't resist sharing in the spur of the moment. And in this instant, Nina is spot on.

The other ladies appear intrigued that Nina has had such a quick and spontaneous turnaround. She has stepped away from her previously held beliefs and has seen something that now makes more sense to her. I have no doubt that the ripples of this insight will continue to serve her in many areas of her life.

> Thanks, Nina, that's really helpful. Let me share something I've learned from my relationship with my own parents. I'm not sure when it all began, but I had expectations of my parents for the longest time. I guess we all do, inevitably failing to see that these expectations are created through Thought. My parents, of course, had no idea what these expectations were. And even if I could have expressed them openly, it's highly unlikely they had the wherewithal to meet them. They were doing their best, just as I do my best to parent my own children.

> Since my early teens, my parents did not seem to understand my inner world and the issues with which I was struggling. So I convinced myself that I could not look to them for the advice and direction which I believed was their duty to provide. Later, when I had emigrated and was married with children, I held on to this conviction. Yes, they were always supportive and loving, but I craved more. When it was not forthcoming, I ended up constantly disappointed that they could not live up to my expectations.

> Because we were living overseas, my mother would come to visit — quite frequently, in fact. But she could not provide the kind of mothering and grandmothering

I wanted. I expected her to be more helpful with the kids and take over in the house so I could relax and have a desperately needed break. I harboured all kinds of thoughts and judgements about my mom enjoying an easier life while I was having a tougher time. I appreciated she was good at listening and empathising but it wasn't enough. I wanted direction, resourcefulness, and hands-on help. But that was simply not her way.

I scan the room, observing in the eyes of my audience recognition and understanding. Mothers, daughters, wives, sisters and friends: they all know what it feels like to have expectations unmet. They know that fortress and how impenetrable it can appear.

Eventually a time came when I was gifted a higher state of consciousness, allowing me to view my parents through different eyes. My parents, I came to appreciate, were genuinely doing the best they could. By now I was 30 years old, but for the first time I was able to love and accept my parents unconditionally. My expectations fell away because thought just dissolves in a higher place of consciousness. If we see life only through our own prism, we have nothing else to guide us but a narrow perspective at a particular juncture.

We cannot do better than the thinking that looks true to us in any given moment. When we arrive at this understanding, our thinking shifts and our unmet expectations of ourselves and others melt away. It leads to a completely different dynamic.

The next time my mother came to visit, I was grateful to relate to her just the way she was. That allowed me to enjoy her without judgement. Similarly with my father. I gave him the freedom — inside my mind — to let him be who he was. Any prior expectations became irrelevant. I placed no demands on them. And I saw that they in no way reduced nor limited my ability to feel joyful, to be connected to life, and to feel love towards them.

My expectations were a product of my own thinking. Once I grasped this, it automatically changed the dynamic between us. This recognition was truly freeing. My parents never changed but *my thinking about them* did. And so my feeling and experience of them did as well.

When my mind was finally unshackled, I understood that any perceived "lack" in my parents was actually my biggest blessing. My parents didn't give me the answers I was seeking because they were not meant to provide them. Since I was not receiving what I believed I needed, I had to rely on my own inner knowing. This is where wisdom truly lies.

An atmosphere of insight and learning permeates the room. As our time together draws to a close, I am, as always, more interested in our feeling, than the content of our discussion.

I know you were hoping for some specific advice, Sharon, but understanding how Thought works *always* explains our experience.

It points to the fact that separate realities exist for each of us. This awareness lies at the heart of understanding our relationships.

Not knowing this creates most — if not all — of the misunderstandings and conflicts in our personal lives and beyond, right up to a global scale. It is one of the core tenets of spiritual and psychological engineering.

When we see that every human being is living from their own creation of Thought, we begin to appreciate how it is impossible to expect others to see the world as we do.

In respecting another person's freedom to see life through their own lens, we realise that it is not only their right, but it is how they were designed and created.

Recognising the truth of separate realities leads us to greater tolerance, acceptance and compassion for our differences. It enables us to reach out, connect and become deeply curious. It facilitates listening intently to others in order to understand their perspective. It gives us a porthole for relating to their reality.

When we appreciate that expectations — no matter how well-founded they may seem — are merely our own thought creations, it frees us to have a different experience of all our relationships. And with that understanding, you won't be looking for prescriptive guidance because *you* will know what to do and how to be.

How does that sound to you, Sharon? Does it resonate?

"Yes, it does," Sharon responds immediately. "I mean, I can see for the first time the role I'm playing in the dynamic with my son. I'd never thought of it like that before. It won't necessarily be easy, but I'd like to try and do things differently starting with recognising how unhelpful my expectations are of him. And I see even more clearly now how my frustration is not coming from him but from me. I can still establish boundaries and educate him. But it's helpful to notice how my upset feeling is coming from Thought — and not from any other source. And you're right, Terry. I *do* know what to do. After all, he's my son and I love him."

I have nothing to add to Sharon's insight. It is time to wrap up.

Before we finish, let me say that understanding the inside-out nature of life is not a technique. It is not a catchy version of positive thinking.

This paradigm is an explanation of the fundamental workings of the mind and the way we experience our entire mental world. Everything we go through can be seen through this understanding: suffering, love, joy, disappointment, stress — you name it.

So the difference between understanding and misunderstanding is enormous. Unless we educate ourselves in the right paradigm, we will constantly feel like a caged bird banging against the bars with no escape. The truth does indeed set you free.

SEARCHING IN THE WRONG PLACE

This is the most common request from those who come to learn: "Tell me what it is and how to do it?" By that they mean: "How do I change my experience; how do I achieve a better, happier state of mind?"

There is no doubt that many are desperate for answers. In a world that is often perplexing and uncomfortable, at times even overwhelming and hostile, people wish to escape stress, anxiety and discomfort. But then they discover that the Principles fail to focus satisfactorily on their specific issues.

What they *do* learn are answers to something else, something unexpected, something fundamental: How does our experience of life work? Where does our thinking come from? What, essentially, is Thought? What determines our state of mind? What are the universal truths that we all share?

And as they develop their own insights around these crucial questions, they often experience a profound shift in their entire psychological, emotional and spiritual experience.

It's strange how we get drawn into the details and lose sight of the bigger picture. As people learn about the Principles, that bigger picture emerges, and then they are able to fill in the details for themselves. It's a bit like when you figure out the borders on a jigsaw puzzle and suddenly the rest of the puzzle falls into place.

Our students and clients come to see that the "answer" they are looking for is not outside of them. It is not an external, elusive, mysterious wisdom that necessitates a great investment of time and effort. It doesn't require a huge intellect, a university degree, a history of personal anguish, years of learning or an entire lifetime of experience.

Psychological well-being is innate. And learning insightfully is natural to all human beings. This is the direction in which the mind flows naturally, like a river flowing with the current. These are the simple laws of the universe.

Deeper knowledge allows people to encounter their own purity of mind. As this occurs, they come to understand that there is nothing to be done. *This is a learning of seeing, not doing*: just like an "aha" moment when everything falls into place. This is what real insight is.

For too long we have sold our souls when it comes to really learning and thinking for ourselves. In our contemporary culture, many of us seek a "how to" approach towards our mental well-being. We believe the myth that so-called experts have the answers and it is up to them to tell us what to do. Many of us end up disillusioned; we try and search and persevere and read and listen — and yet still we do not find the answers we are seeking.

But that is because we are naively searching in the wrong place. In a world of information overload, we are accustomed to grabbing bits and pieces of advice from many sources. We then attempt to cobble them all together, hoping they will translate into specific changes in our habits and behaviours.

Every time I glimpse the bigger picture or the oneness of life, the "what" and "how" questions become redundant. When I lose myself in the fragmentation of my analytic mind and the tangled web of my thoughts, I search fruitlessly for answers to fix my inner and outer worlds. But when I descend into the space of truth, which lies beyond any fragmentation of thought and form, everything emerges effortlessly. There is a perfect unfolding, without judgement, without confusion and without distress. The whole is indeed greater than the sum of its parts. You simply cannot understand or grasp the separate parts without seeing everything in the context of the whole.

Mind, Consciousness and Thought provide us with the simplest gateway to glimpse the whole. This is ultimately where answers arise and clarity dawns. Rather than going after answers like a child chasing an elusive butterfly, they will find us if we quiet down enough to let that happen.

And when they do, when that beautiful butterfly lands gently on our hearts and souls, this wonderful world lived from the inside-out will never look more divine.

PART III
LIVING
WITH UNDERSTANDING

"As we start to regain the true relationship between our personal intelligence and the spiritual wisdom that lies within, we develop a higher degree of intelligence and common sense. This, in turn, clears up our misguided lives."

Sydney Banks

"The most beautiful thing we can experience is the mysterious; it is the source of all true art and science. When the solution is simple, God is answering."

Albert Einstein

6

NEVER-ENDING LEARNING[5]

LIVING LIFE'S UPS AND DOWNS
WITH MORE GRACE

One of the most common misunderstandings is to assume that the Principles will lead to a steady stream of positive, happy thoughts — even, perhaps, to an oasis of peace of mind. To believe this is to misconstrue the nature of experience.

My own journey of learning about the Principles has not always been straightforward. Once I recovered from the Great Depression and even before coming across the Principles, I experienced a completely fresh state of mind that was novel to me. This paved the way for much energised and exhilarating thinking. Like a baby enjoying every waking moment, I felt stimulated and excited about life and my potential. I was not conscious of any negative feelings — they just didn't seem to visit me. Everything felt so open

---

[5] Part III shows how this revolutionary new understanding has played out for me in real life situations over the past decade. My intention is to demonstrate how three simple but fundamental spiritual facts have enormously powerful and practical implications in everyday life. I advise you to view what I share as a gateway to seeing the implications of the teachings we explored in Part II. So don't get stuck on whether you agree or don't agree with how my life played out - you have enough to worry about.

and light. I was like the man — or woman — on the moon, having a surreal, buoyant, uplifting experience that defied the gravitational pull of real existence on earth. And yet, I was more engaged in day-to-day life than ever.

But then there came a time when I started to struggle more. Not struggle in the sense that I sank back into depression or became my old anxious self. I simply felt more fear or frustration than usual. I became increasingly irritated with Brian; preoccupied with keeping the house spotlessly clean; concerned that I wasn't successfully managing the balance of being both a working woman and mother. Even though I could recognise what was occurring — merely Thought streaming through my system creating my feeling state — I was no longer accustomed to these more uncomfortable feelings. I needed to be patient.

Over the years, I've seen the same phenomenon happen to many clients and students. When people first learn about who they really are and understand their own innate health; when they see how the whole system works and learn to appreciate the nature of Thought; when they are able to ascend to a deeper, richer feeling, they initially enjoy a magical, perhaps even euphoric, sense of well-being. Unrestricted and unattached, they no longer feel trapped.

And then their thinking starts to get really sneaky, creeping up on them like a mischievous prankster when they least expect it. They become frightened. "Are the Principles not working?" they ask. (As if principles, which by definition are constant, can ever stop working.) They assume that fear, anxiety, frustration and anger have been permanently banished. They think they will never feel bad again and are often shocked and distressed when they do.

But this is simply not the way the system works. Nobody ever declared that the Principles are the pathway to a perfect existence. They do not provide some kind of invisible vaccination, creating instant immunity against a whole range of emotions.

The Principles uncover the human experience and reveal that we have nothing from which we need to "protect" ourselves. There is nothing to avoid, nothing to change or fear. Life need not be perfect when we gain perspective and can see the bigger picture.

June, 2010

Intense feelings of being down — the strongest I've had since I learned about the Principles — are coursing through me. They are accompanied by compelling thoughts that what I'm feeling is too painful and difficult; that it's all too much; that I need to escape. It's a déjà vu experience, catapulting me back to a place I hoped I had left far behind.

And before I know it, my thoughts are running wild.

Who am I kidding? These Principles and what I've learned are just rubbish; they are nonsense. They aren't substantial enough to contain the feelings I'm experiencing right now. This is too big, too real, and my understanding of the Principles can't help me weather this storm.

Just as my thinking is tightening its stranglehold, a deeper knowing emerges. I laugh to myself at how absurd my internal dialogue sounds. It's as though I'm irritated, even a little resentful, of the truth I have learned. Because I know that nothing else can change my chemistry as it has over these last couple of days. Only Thought can do that. I've seen it before and I know it to be true.

My ego wants to dismiss this understanding and wallow in a cycle of unhelpful thinking. I want to medicate the negative feelings and be a depressive again (for a couple of hours, at least). But I simply cannot. Why? Because I have acquired a deep inner knowing. 1+1=2. My thoughts are creating these feelings: that's the sum of it. I know where my mental experience is coming from.

And that's what happens when you meet true knowledge. You can't turn your back on it. I couldn't. What I had previously thought was true was certainly not, and from now on, I have to live faithfully with what I know.

My understanding of the nature of those old yet still familiar feelings *was* true because a few days later I *was* doing better. Unlike the past, my low mood now did lift.

Previously, I would have become attached to these feelings, treated them as sacrosanct and felt frightened by their power. But now, the small slither of consciousness that had brought forth my understanding yielded a new experience. And it made all the difference. What could potentially have been the onset of a depressive episode was now no more than a sensory experience that soon passed through my system.

I have come to embrace the inevitable "whack" I get when things aren't quite going the way I expect — and the powerful dose of humility that always accompanies it. I have never thought of myself as a person with a big ego, but that's not the point. We all have an ego, and we could all do with becoming more humble. The fact that I struggle at times has its blessings. It brings me down a few notches, provides a blunt reminder: *You're not so enlightened, girl! There's a big bundle of thinking that feels very real to you. You haven't seen everything you need to see. There's a great deal of learning you still have to undertake, a world of knowledge still waiting to be accessed.*

This reminder helps me cherish my "humanness". It helps me appreciate what I still need to learn. It helps me relate to people around me. It helps me understand what my husband and sons and brother and sister and parents and friends and colleagues and clients and so many others are going through. We are all human and in the same boat and learning all of the time. And we are all doing just fine.

It also enables me to cherish my resilience. No matter what I am going through, I feel anchored and secure. I am not thrown off course by fluctuations in my thinking. I am merely swayed a little, notwithstanding my anxiety, fear, despair or other emotions.

From the earliest age, I went through ups and downs; moments of elation and moments of disappointment. And I still do. Nobody escapes these moments. It's simply the natural way of life.

Living the human experience with this perspective is priceless. It always sets us straight, helping us through the normal vicissitudes of life with grace and equanimity.

STEPPING OUTSIDE
OUR CONDITIONED THINKING

As the number of people who have been touched by the Principles has grown exponentially, remarkable stories of transformation have emerged. Many who experienced years of mental anguish, caught in the interminable cycle of depression and anxiety, arrived at lasting mental well-being. Men and women struggling with eating disorders, chronically low self-esteem, dysfunctional relationships, severe phobias and other mental health challenges have all made substantial progress.

And then there are those simply grappling with a host of day-to-day life issues. Husbands and wives resolve years of irreconcilable conflicts. Parents describe a transformation in their parenting approach and relationship to their children. Teachers confirm a radically enhanced experience of their students and the classroom dynamic. Teenagers talk about a greater sense of security and better self-esteem. Psychologists, executive coaches, community and business leaders have all come to learn with us. A high proportion of them are touched by what they hear; some integrate the Principles into their practices, organisations and communities. Indeed, we are beginning to notice the impact of the Principles in all walks of life.

This is also evident in businesspeople and entrepreneurs who attribute significant commercial upturns and improved productivity of their employees to what they are learning. Here is one example...

"A treasure chest of gold in my own backyard"
James' insight

A few years back, I was in a tough position with the business I had started. I was unbelievably hectic, busy to distraction, running around like a headless chicken. In a way it felt good that I was so busy. But at the same time, I knew that there was something lacking: I was not nearly as productive, effective or creative as I could be. No matter how much effort I applied, the output did not seem to justify the input.

The business began to struggle. Problems were appearing everywhere I turned: with investors, partners, clients, colleagues, suppliers — you name it. My life had become a nightmare. I reached a point where my mind felt like it was spinning 24/7. This had a major impact on my entire life: at work, at home, in relationships. It was really tough trying to spin so many plates; I became fearful everything would come crashing down. But I didn't have a clue what to do about it other than to keep on with the intensity, the busyness, the running around.

No matter how hard I tried, I wasn't finding solutions and my desperation began to spiral. So when Grant, our new Operations Director, suggested I meet up with a fellow named Aaron of One Thought, who specialised in helping entrepreneurs become more effective, I agreed straight away. I knew nothing about the kind of work this man did but I — and the business — had reached a stage of near-collapse. So I was willing to try just about anything.

I spent four days switching off, settling down, and opening up — the stuff that happens when you just let yourself be. And it really unleashed something quite amazing. I had all these epiphanies and mental and physical highs over those four days.

I realised something that was patently obvious and yet concealed: the knowledge that I have a deep quiet place within, where wisdom and solutions reside. It was as if a light bulb was suddenly switched on: *What, this is how it works? Oh, my God! I didn't even know it was there!* There's that old story of the goldmine in the guy's back yard. He was searching for gold everywhere but it was right under his nose the whole time. How the heck is it possible that this understanding was there in the first place?

And here's the fantastic thing: you don't have to switch anything on. It's more like you have to *not* switch it on. The less you do, the more you are likely to achieve. I know it sounds paradoxical, counterintuitive, and the antithesis of everything we've been taught. This is why the term "innate" is an apt designation. A Western education and approach is all about looking for lessons and information outside oneself, as opposed to that which is lodged within.

Prior to working with Aaron, I spent copious hours worrying about raising funds for the business. Thoughts swirled endlessly in my head, keeping me up most nights. In a fast-growth enterprise, you need fuel for the fire. Most entrepreneurs face this same challenge: how to expand rapidly without emptying the coffers. It's my job to ensure this doesn't happen, but concurrently we need to grow and push forward. So it is not surprising that they kept me awake.

Once I was exposed to the Principles, my anxiety lessened. I had more of what you might call "faith"; trust in myself that I would know how to react and how to steer the business in the right direction. I learned to relax for the first time in years, perhaps ever. As I calmed down, I began to grasp the potential of Mind to deliver the right solution when I needed. I saw that if I was willing to listen, the answers would present themselves. That was an incredible revelation.

The implicit but false contract you have with yourself is that if you spend enough time thinking about something, you'll find the right answer. Recognising that over-analysis and round-the-clock thinking is not the correct pathway was perhaps the most important lesson I have ever learned.

This has given me both a mental and physical freedom that has been absolutely game-changing. I saw that everything — every single thing — comes from within. As a consequence, I realised I could and would cope with a host of matters that had previously seemed unmanageable. I understood now that I was creating my own reality, with the result that my issues were no longer such a big deal. I could actually work them out really well. Infinite possibilities and great wisdom had become available.

I now feel clearer and wiser about myself and the business. With every passing month there's been a significant shift in what is achievable. I have freed myself from a reliance on old thinking that everything is coming from the outside. I know now that the solutions to our "problems" are within. As long as I retain faith in myself, and stick to seeking out that inner quiet place, both I — and the business — will realise enormous potential.

We've achieved so much more in the past three years than in the previous fifteen. The business is growing easily and expanding, we're making money, and we've got fantastic partners. At the same time, I'm enjoying more freedom than ever before.

And to think that the answer was there all the time: a treasure chest of gold in my own backyard.

A DEEPER KNOWING

Call us a little crazy, but Brian and I had always wanted to have a large, bustling family. We were blessed with five sons, but we still harboured a strong desire to have a daughter.

Despite this yearning, I was fully immersed in the joy of watching the boys grow up. It was fulfilling and fun parenting these five emerging souls, each with their own distinct personalities, traits, talents, temperaments and tantrums. And I also loved the wonderful work to which I was committed. Yet neither Brian nor I were quite ready to give up on expanding our family. We were becoming increasingly conscious that almost eight years after Daniel's birth, the age gap was widening by the month. If we didn't want to close the door entirely on the option of another child, we needed to move towards a decision.

But the necessary clarity eluded us. Our deliberations were compounded by the very strong likelihood that another Rubenstein baby would mean, as had been the case with his brothers, chronic digestive problems for the first couple of years. Inevitably, this would be accompanied by endless crying, many sleepless nights and exhausting, trying days. Rubenstein babies already had a bad reputation amongst those who knew us well. (Although in their defence, it must be noted that none of them had ever robbed a bank or drowned a stray cat — at least not to our knowledge.)

The more we talked about another child, the more a web of confusion enveloped us. We thought about it and thought about it some more, tossing seemingly endless considerations back and forth. We asked the opinion of those whose advice we valued; we carefully considered every angle. And still the clarity did not come. So, no closer to resolving the matter, I met with Aaron Turner, my old mentor, one afternoon at the Costa coffee shop around the corner from our offices. After giving him the lowdown, I asked the obvious question:

"Why am I getting so stuck about this choice? Why is it so difficult to arrive at a decision?"

"Well, Terry, why try make a decision from a place of confusion?" Aaron asked in his inimical way in between sipping from his extra-large cappuccino.

This was typical Aaron — straight to the point, cutting through the small talk and shedding light on the heart of the issue.

The insight wrapped around me like a comforting blanket. Aaron was absolutely right: it didn't make any sense to act out of a confused mind. I was teaching this very idea in my classes, sharing it with my clients. But up close and personal with my own thinking, this insight had eluded me — until now.

It struck me in that moment that I did not know the right way to proceed. And so, as clarity failed to materialise, I chose not to act. I was well aware that too much personal thinking was clouding my mind. As long as that existed, I could not and would not gain clarity. And I simply was not prepared to make a choice from a state of mind that I neither trusted nor respected.

A place exists for us all where we know with certainty what to do and how the next stage of life is meant to unfold. It is the place where wisdom and clarity meet. There is no doubt or confusion when that moment arrives, only a deep sense of knowing.

At this time, I also arrived at an invaluable insight. I realised that no matter what decisions I make — even if they seem to be wrong ones — I will always have access to my own well-being. This applies irrespective of the actual decision itself. My well-being is an innate, unconditional gift that does not disappear when I make poor choices. Crucially, this allows me to feel free and psychologically safe to make "mistakes" along the way.

About six months later, the unexpected happened. We were enjoying a summer holiday in Cornwall with close friends who also had a large family. Something about those two quiet weeks with another large, lively family in the beautiful English countryside created a surprising shift within me...

August, 2010

It is a glorious summer's evening. The setting sun casts dancing shadows across the high wooden ceilings of the lovely old farmhouse we are renting. Suddenly, I am struck by a moment of clarity. I am downstairs putting things away in the kitchen, but I rush in search of my husband with a swift sense of purpose. There is something important I need to tell him.

Brian is upstairs in the cavernous bedroom.

"What's up?" he asks casually, completely oblivious to the bombshell I am about to drop.

"We're going to have another baby."

That got his attention! After a few moments of stunned silence, my man of many words manages to fashion a highly eloquent response.

"Really?"

"Yep!"

"Uh, OK. Thanks for letting me know."

And that was it. Brian knew instantly I had arrived at clarity. It just felt right. No thinking came with that feeling. All doubt had gone. No amount of subsequent thinking could persuade me otherwise — despite the fears and concerns that intermittently appeared in the ensuing months. From that moment on, irrespective whether we would have a girl or not, we went along with that decision as if it was the only one we could possibly have made.

Now, a few short years later, we are blessed with the most beautiful little boy who is fast approaching his fourth birthday and has us all wrapped adoringly around his tiny fingers. It is impossible for Brian or me or any of his doting brothers to contemplate any reality other than one which includes precious Mikey in our lives. Even though we endured 20 trying months of little sleep and constant crying; even though we had countless and often futile visits to paediatricians and specialists to alleviate his chronic cramping; even though it proved hard to resume work; and even though I often feel wrenched from my little boy because of my busy job, there is absolutely no doubt that choosing to have Mikey was the best decision we ever made.

The process of learning comes in many guises. We have seen that one of the most powerful, effective ways for a person to learn about the Principles occurs when they are able to step outside the previous beliefs of their conditioned minds. This enables them to experience a sufficiently quiet space, which helps deeper insight to flourish. A four-day "intensive" is the ideal opportunity for that to occur...

"When my mind is quiet,
I can hear my own answers"
Shelly's intensive

So here's the thing: I'm not quite sure what I was doing there in the first place, talking to a woman whom I had only met briefly once before. Not only that, but I had committed four days of my life to this "conversation".

This was a most uncharacteristic thing for me to do. I was a recently qualified GP leading a busy life, leaving little time to contemplate my own psychological well-being. But on a recent holiday in Majorca, a friend had told me how much he had benefitted from his own intensive. And despite my robust efforts to project myself as a successful, fulfilled career woman, a very different picture existed inside.

Terry began with what she called "intake": a brief biographical sketch and summary of where I was up to at that stage in my life. I saw no point in holding back, so I shared my recent trauma. An intense, serious relationship had ended, leaving me fragile and vulnerable. Not long after, I was raped. Acute flashbacks to that event were taking their toll on my mind and body. I managed to conceal what I was going through, but I was in a lot of inner pain.

To my surprise, Terry didn't press for any details. She didn't probe into my childhood or the recesses of my memory. Although there was compassion in her eyes and genuine empathy in her voice, she was more interested in steering the conversation in another direction.

When I arrived the next morning, I told Terry about the multitude of thoughts swirling around my head since the previous session. Terry simply stated that this is the nature of the human experience. She went on to explain how Thought works and its relationship to feelings.

As we spoke, it occurred to me that there were instances when I felt great.

"This seems to happen when I receive a compliment from a stranger or during a first meeting with someone I had never met before," I explained. "In those moments, I have no preconceived notions and nothing to fear, so these strangers are merely reflecting my positivity back at me. And I realise now that it is not because of them that I feel good — it is because of me! During these encounters, my soul is at its best, most natural, formless state."

Talking with Terry, I understood that the positive feelings I felt towards comparative strangers could be generated towards anyone. I had the power to shift my relationships, whether with patients, colleagues or members of my family. I realised that if I could generate self-kindness and self-compassion, then I could also share it. The frustration and exhaustion "caused" by many of my patients could dissolve. Now that I realised it was self-created, the resentment I so often felt towards others need not hold me in its powerful grip.

During the lunch break on Day Three, I retreated to a softly-lit room within the Innate Health Centre and listened to a CD by Sydney Banks. He was talking about the value of a quiet mind in his lilting Scottish accent and calming voice. "Everyone in this world shares the same source of innate wisdom, but it is hidden by the tangle of our own misguided thoughts."

My thoughts had controlled me for as long as I could remember. Now, for the first time, I understood that in spite of the painful feelings and memories, I need not cleave to them. I had the free will to disengage from the powerful attachment to my thoughts. It was such a gift to arrive at this realisation.

Halfway through the afternoon session, I found myself voluntarily talking about the rape. The veil was lifting; I could adopt a different approach. I had been suffering for too long. And my thoughts were taking me there. As soon as this realisation sunk in, the flashbacks stopped eliciting such an overt physical and emotional response. Given time, I sensed the flashbacks would reduce in frequency and intensity.

I walked out of the Centre at the end of Day Three, full of hope and clarity. I was really looking forward to what my final day would uncover...

The next day I didn't wait for Terry to begin. I jumped straight in, eager to share the insights percolating in my mind.

"Something that happens to us remains a part of our thoughts as long as we allow it to," I told Terry.

"Previously, I felt I had no control over the impact of unhappy memories; I was distressed by them, and desperate for change. The realisation that they are my own thoughts causing this state of mind allows me to regain control of my day-to-day experience."

Sitting on the other side of the simple, wooden coffee table, Terry simply nodded, encouraging me to continue.

"I've always assumed that someone reacts a certain way because of me — something I've said or done. But I understand now that it actually has nothing to do with me. It's a result of another's thinking. What I am feeling is always because of my own reality that I have constructed. And the same goes for others. We are all living in our separate realities."

When we returned for the final afternoon session, I wanted to explore an issue that remained unresolved since I had qualified as a GP: the next phase of my medical career.

"I keep trying to figure out a plan for what's next but I just land up with so much noise in my head and can't get any clarity. It's so frustrating," I complained.

"We've spent almost four days slowing down," Terry replied. "Your mind is so quiet compared to the beginning of the week. You have an understanding now of how Thought works and how it can speed you up. You've touched the feeling that accompanies self-insight; that feeling which says that only you know what makes perfect sense for yourself."

Terry paused for a long moment. "So what is that answer that lies inside of you, Shelly?"

I didn't miss a beat in responding: "Nothing! I have no plan for the next stage of my career. I just want to let it take its natural course."

A huge wave of relief and inner confidence came over me as I uttered these words. Since then, I keep going back to that place whenever I am confused or have moments of doubt. Because I know that when my mind is quiet, I can hear my own answers.

This is so exciting; it is such progress for me. It is not a miracle cure. I never expected some kind of voodoo magic. But it was wonderful to realise, at the end of my intensive, that I had gained an understanding. I know this will always guide me as I go through the inevitable ups and downs, and questions and answers of life.

AN OPEN MIND KEEPS ON LEARNING

When it comes to learning about the Principles, it is crucial to recognise that the process is not linear. It is not about following a series of steps, one after the other, to acquire knowledge.

Far more important is the depth of a person's "grounding". By that I mean how an understanding of Mind, Consciousness and Thought seeps into our entire psychological experience.

> **The more grounded we are, the more that will reflect itself in our day-to-day living. So learning is not about *knowing more* — but about learning *deeper*.**

The principle of gravity tells us something fundamental about how physics operates: all matter is dragged downwards by gravitational force. It's a natural law of the universe. And it's best not to disregard this principle. Because if I do, when I roll out of bed in the morning, I'm bound to land on the floor.

So too with "psychological grounding". It requires going back to the paradigm and asking: Are the Principles merely useful concepts standing me in good stead while I reframe my thinking? Or do they denote something more fundamental? Are they inviolable natural laws that explain the entire human experience? Am I open to the possibility that this understanding could lead to a profound shift in my relationship to life?

Unlike the earth's gravitational pull, the Principles of Mind, Consciousness and Thought are easier to disregard. They are less obvious to us — at least initially. Frequently and repeatedly, we lose sight of them. At such times we find ourselves rolling out of our metaphorical beds and bumping our heads on the floor. We have lost, at least temporarily, our psychological way. We fall into a trap of misunderstanding.

We attribute our feelings to something other than our thinking in the moment. We forget that everything is just Thought, brought to life through Consciousness, which creates our felt experience of life.

When this occurs there is nothing more important to remember than this: just as our physical bodies are designed to fall asleep and wake up, the same applies psychologically and spiritually.

The capacity for ongoing learning is a feature of the human condition. Intrinsic to this process is remaining in a constant state of curiosity. For adults, this may be difficult to achieve. For young children, it comes naturally and with an effortless ease. So whenever I wonder whether I am slowing down in my learning, I find myself looking towards little Mikey for guidance.

For several months, our youngest son has watched the same DVD while eating his breakfast every morning. He never seems to get bored with Peppa Pig, Miss Rabbit and their furry friends. It may seem like Groundhog Day to the rest of us every time the theme music from his favourite programme starts up, but not to him. Yet a time is coming that I fear is not far away. It is the day when my little boy switches off the mini-DVD player perched precariously on the edge of his highchair, turns to me and says: "Mommy, I don't want to watch Peppa Pig anymore. I'm tired of it. I've seen it before."

In common with most small children, Mikey is blessed with a natural, innate ability to learn. He will watch the same simple programme over and over again. Yet still he remains curious, retaining a heightened state of fascination. He wants to know more, to learn and to absorb. This is a capacity that I took for granted as a young child, and which I slowly but surely lost as I grew older and "matured".

There was a time when we learnt huge amounts with little or no effort. Almost by osmosis, we absorbed from our environment as effortlessly as a child is nourished in the womb. We had an enthusiasm and energy for learning anew. We were alive in the present moment; we enjoyed a natural and boundless curiosity to understand the world around us.

But when our analytic and sophisticated thought systems begin to develop, we often lose respect for that childlike wonder. Unwittingly, the intellect starts to suffocate our innate intelligence, an intelligence that learns on its own, that is guided by the natural wisdom of the mind.

We assume we know and stop being curious about what we don't know. We forget that we have a constant river of fresh thinking flowing through our minds, touching our souls and coming to life as new learning.

My understanding of the Principles has helped me to appreciate the secret quality that enables my four-year-old to continually watch and learn from Peppa time and again. Yes, the day will dawn when he will have had enough. But I have no doubt when that occurs he too will learn the power of dipping into his spiritual wellspring. He too will access the resourceful energy that allows us to re-create, to re-learn and to see life afresh, again and again.

That is the wondrous, innate capacity with which we are all endowed: a capacity that will always afford us access to the never-ending learning that is one of the most precious gifts of an exquisite mind.

WE HAVE EVERYTHING WE NEED

Because of our perceived flaws, weaknesses and inconsistent behaviours, human beings may appear to be lacking something. But an understanding of the Principles shows that every person has what is needed, all the resources required to fully engage with life.

This includes, of course, our own children. It goes without saying that my boys require a great deal from me: to start with, copious amounts of food, homework help, medical appointments and everything else associated with their daily needs and running a functional home. Each child also requires a specific balance of love, guidance, direction and support according to their individual temperaments and dispositions. What the Principles have taught me is that even when I don't get all of these elements right — and for sure I don't all of the time — the kids are still going to be just fine. They are always connected to wisdom and common sense, always linked to the guiding intelligence of the universe. Once I had seen this for myself, it was an enormous relief, a huge burden lifted off my shoulders.

It's been a long while since I felt any compulsion to make my kids perfect. They are creating their own particular reality through their own free will. They are walking their own fascinating journey. They will have times when they will lose their way. And then there will be other moments when they find the right path again.

My role is a much gentler one. I need not over-parent nor, like a helicopter mom, hover anxiously. I watch them, trust them, enjoy them and offer my own wisdom when it feels right to do so. My own learning was a bumpy ride, and though there were some pretty big ups and some painful downs along the way, I got there in the end. So I know they will too.

The boys appreciate it when I respect their own inner wisdom. They love it when I let them experience the fullness of life's joys and disappointments without jumping in to fix matters or change their own creations. They enjoy learning that their frailties and failures are all part of this "game of life". They are grateful for having the freedom to create anew in each moment and not be judged for the previous one. And they love knowing that I retain faith in the buoyancy of their well-being to bring them back to their true selves, even when that seems temporarily lost.

Each of the boys is handling his own experiences with greater or lesser intensity and grace, depending on his state of mind. As their mother, I observe with awe and humility six beautiful, capable and resourceful souls drawing on their own wisdom and common sense. How perfect they seem, given the knowledge I have of the wholeness of each one.

> **Parenting from such a broad perspective, where there is an appreciation of the truth underlying the human experience, allows us to let our children be. We may gently steer them if necessary, but we give ourselves the freedom to trust in our kids' own conscience and inner knowledge.**

This approach permits us to see the innocence that lies behind our children's thinking should it lead them astray.

Failing to see this potential in our children is the cause of much insecurity and anxiety in parents — and, of course, in children themselves.

December, 2012

One of the teenagers has come home from school late this wintry afternoon. He is going through a rough period, but today he seems even angrier than usual. Before I know it, he starts ripping up a photo album depicting a recent family celebration.

He is tearing it apart, throwing the photos all over the floor. I am not sure how to deal with him. I don't even tell him to put it down because I can see he is not going to listen to me. I can't believe he has come home and reacted like this. Only this morning, before he left, I was so attentive, making his favourite sandwich for lunch and promising to take him shopping later for new trainers.

Suddenly I become aware of how frustrated I am. I catch the feeling. I notice that my mind is filled with thinking.

Acknowledging that this feeling is coming from within me, and not from his actions, I am able to turn away from it. The process is effortless. Within seconds I quiet down and find myself speaking in a very assertive tone:

"Put that album down! I don't want you to destroy it."

He is highly agitated and keeps shouting at me. But he puts the album down straight away, which really surprises me.

Then something occurs to me: "You need to eat," I say.

And I place a bowl of fresh pasta in front of him. I don't normally do that with my kids. He's a big boy and he doesn't usually need me to encourage him to eat.

"I forgot my lunch this morning; I'm starving," he mumbles angrily.

He reaches for the food and starts eating. Soon, his whole body relaxes. I gently put my hand on his shoulder and he immediately starts to sob. Within minutes, all of the energy goes out of the incident and I feel deeply connected to him.

It was such a powerful experience for the very reason it was a normal, everyday, mothering occurrence. But the change was so simple that I could have missed it. It was only when I saw where my frustration was coming from that my head cleared and I knew what to do. Until that moment, I didn't know how to handle the situation. How was I going to get him to calm down, to stop being so destructive? He was unlikely to listen to reason, so what else was I going to say or do? I was unsure if he needed me to be firm or soft with him: did he need love or boundaries at that particular moment?

Yet the amazing thing is that we are connected to an intelligence that *does* know what to do. I could say what I did in an assertive tone which derived from a neutral feeling, not from an angry one. And it worked. Not only that, but out of nowhere it occurred to me to do something I virtually never do — tell him to eat.

Just that bit of guidance makes all the difference: it gives you faith that you are not alone in figuring out what to do. It is most reassuring to know that you are operating in a system which is larger than you, connected to a Mind that knows what you cannot know.

LESSONS IN LISTENING AND LOVE

Being interested in what we don't know — as opposed to what we do already know — is the true gateway to deeper learning. This facilitates deep listening, which opens up a porthole for genuine connection and understanding.

This kind of listening is not an action that is performed. It extends well beyond giving someone undivided attention and focus.

Real listening occurs when we are not distracted or diverted by our own thinking. We know that when we quiet down sufficiently, when we are present in the moment, we reach beyond the content of the spoken word or the specific behaviour. This then allows us to hear the underlying intent and tune into another's feeling.

When it comes to my children, I often find myself asking: "What is his state of mind?" One boy might be hitting another, or being rude, or completely ignoring my impassioned pleas not to walk upstairs with his muddy shoes. Outwardly, he appears to be obstructive, destructive or indifferent (and sometimes a combination of all three!). But inside, he may well be anxious about an exam tomorrow. My job, as their mother, is to see beyond the immediate behaviour in order to understand what is really going on inside. And when I am able to do that, I acquire an appreciation of their state of mind. I become helpful, directive, firm, empathetic, or whatever else is needed to be supportive in that situation.

My boys, just like the rest of us, are simply acting out their moment-to-moment states of mind. Some of them don't yet have the maturity to fully understand — or the capacity to tell us — what is going on in their hearts and minds. So we, as parents, rely on preconditioned assumptions, leading to the kind of thinking that says: *Here he goes again; he always does that; I know this kid.*

> **But when we go beyond the attachment to the constant commentary in our minds, we are able to hear something besides our own judgemental and personal views. We can discern that which is hidden from us and our children. This applies to all human beings.**

A genuine place of listening is both practical and helpful. You see the innocence underlying someone's actions; you understand where they are coming from; you realise that behaviour is simply a reflection of a person's thinking in the moment.

This is very connecting. You are doing more than hearing the content or the information. You are listening at an intuitive level. By absorbing the entire context, you are really listening to another. When this happens — when you move beyond the actual words — you genuinely connect, gaining a strong rapport and deeper insight into what is *actually* going on.

Having reached his teenage years, Josh lost his way for a while. Almost overnight, a whole range of issues and emotions began colliding. He quickly transitioned from being an easy-going, playful child to a distraught, angry and down-in-the-dumps adolescent. There were dented doors and difficult days when he refused to go to school. Highly charged emotional outbursts and teenage tantrums became part of the daily routine.

Yet though his behaviour was fairly extreme, and there were moments where I was exasperated by it, I had no doubt he'd be all right. Perhaps most importantly, I loved him (most of the time!) even though his behaviour was often unlovable. And I made sure that he knew that — and knew the difference.

My message to him was this: "There is nothing wrong with you. You'll be fine. Life can be challenging at times but you have the resources you need to cope; there are things you can and will learn and you are able to get through this."

I wanted him to know that it's normal and natural to go through ups and downs, and he need not be afraid. My own adolescence was full of trauma and confusion. Lacking any context or explanation for my emotions, I often felt vulnerable and inadequate. Now, as a mother, my role was to reassure him that he had the inner resources to find his own path. And to support him in whatever way I could. Critically, I did not do this from a place of anxiety or fear for my son. I was able to guide him using common sense and a clear mind.

Slowly but surely Josh started to emerge from his low moods and explosions of rage. He began to understand the role that he was playing in creating his own turmoil. He stopped seeing himself as a victim and ceased laying the blame on the school, his brothers and other external factors. To the everlasting relief of the entire family (some of his outbursts were loud and long enough to even upset the equilibrium of our testosterone-filled home), he experienced a remarkable turnaround.

One of the most important lessons I learned through Josh was the unspoken expectations he felt were placed on him.

He was in the tough position of following two older brothers who were doing well, both in school and extra-curricular activities. I had conveyed to Josh on many occasions that there was no need to measure up to them, that he was his own special person and that I cherished him. Nonetheless, I must have unconsciously communicated the message that he still needed to be exceptional, albeit in a different way.

One day Josh confronted me, wanting to know why I had these expectations. At first I attempted to defend myself. I had deliberately tried not to formulate any expectations, having made a conscious effort to avoid any comparisons with his older brothers.

And then mid-conversation, I caught myself. It was the feeling that woke me up. The ego mind has a feeling to it which is tight and defensive. I realised in that moment that I *did* have expectations of Josh — just different, shifted expectations. I stopped trying to defend myself. Instead, I backed away from my thinking. It was a startling instant of catching my ego at work.

The beauty of being able to let go of certain thoughts is that they are instantly replaced by new thoughts without us having to do anything. An understanding of the role Thought plays is the key to unlocking our expectations and freeing us from our narrow constraints.

It was this understanding that allowed me to turn towards my son and say: "You're right, Josh, I'm really sorry. I *do* have expectations. But I just wasn't aware of them, and that's not helpful or fair to you."

From then on, I shifted to a new level of unconditional love for my son. I let Josh be himself, although that was at odds with my own perception of how a teenager should be. I had been constrained by my attitudes, applying them unhelpfully to Josh. Once I realigned my position, I could show Josh that I trusted in his capacity to access his own wisdom and travel his own unique path. This was a game-changer for us both.

Because Josh could now sense that unconditional love, he blossomed. He reconnected with me and in so doing, I gained the capacity to influence and guide him as I had when he was younger and less independent. I could be assertive and firm with him when appropriate because he knew that my guiding hand was coming from a place of love, compassion and trust.

Unsurprisingly, our children seem to respect boundaries and direction if they know it's coming from a place of love as opposed to a place of frustration or judgement.

Josh is doing just fine now. Part of his healthy functioning may have gone missing for a while, but he was never really lost. Knowing that is one of the greatest lessons of his young life. And unexpectedly, he has become one of my best teachers.

"Keep calm. It's only an extra chromosome"
Jenna's "special" kids

There was a time when I was completely overwhelmed as a parent. I guess you could say that my circumstances justified my struggles. We have five children including two who have "special needs", plus our adopted daughter who has Down's syndrome. To compound matters, not long after the adoption, we were stunned by the news that my daughter's heart was in very bad shape. She required major heart surgery.

We were surrounded by lots of well-meaning professionals who led us to believe the situation was dire. They told us we should be grieving, we should expect to be in a state of conflict, we should barely be able to keep our heads above water. The "experts" were very kind and supportive. But there was an unavoidable underlying message: "We are the professionals coming in to show you how to live your life."

At the same time, I was reading every parenting manual, special needs book and article I could. I consulted with many specialists. And I discovered they shared a common premise: children need to be treated differently — all the more so in the case of special needs kids. And we, the parents, are in urgent need of help. By this time I was a successful professional, having reached management positions as a teacher before the age of 30. Yet I unquestioningly accepted their distinction between disabled and non-disabled kids.

I felt I was failing as a mother, drowning on all fronts. I soon gave up my career. In my state of despondency, my children were simply a collection of symptoms with no hope in sight. Frustrated and confused, I found myself in continuous conflict with the various services and institutions offering help and support.

Eventually my husband turned to me one day and said:

"Jenna, we could lock you in a room on your own and you would have a fight with yourself. Why don't you get help, go for counselling?"

This was a pivotal moment. "No!" I replied emphatically. I intuitively understood that therapy wasn't the answer to my problems.

I sensed that suffering wasn't meant to be so immense; that there must be some other way of managing life's huge challenges. Surely I could do so with more grace and less effort? But I was unaware how to change things for myself.

And then, if you believe in coincidences, I stumbled on the Principles. I heard a talk at my kids' school from an Innate Health practitioner. *Hmmm, what she is speaking about sounds like it may be of help,* I thought. I decided to attend a Parenting course at the Innate Health Centre in North West London. And before long, I started to see things differently.

It took time for the insights and the teachings to hit home. There was no overnight transformation. But as I began to get a handle on my own psychological functioning, I realised that it wasn't just me getting caught up in my thoughts — it was everybody. And that included all my children — those with "special needs" as well as those without.

Despite being really good at attending meetings, filling out dozens of forms and managing, if not micro-managing their lives, it struck me that I didn't know my own kids all that well. This was a major insight. The "experts" asserted that the children and I were very different. But I realised that this wasn't the case. They were doing the same things as I: living their experience through their thoughts.

This understanding enabled me to become more accepting and less judgemental of the children's efforts. When they are down, they act out, just as I do. When they are doing better, it's good for us all and we make some progress. Or, maybe it's neither. Then we just hang out together and eat potato crisps. I don't need to judge any of these states — they are all good options.

For the first time, I had a feeling of kinship with my "disabled" kids. I started to see beyond the labels. It was a joy to get to know them and realise they are creative, funny, and intelligent. And also annoying, frustrating and exhausting — just like my other kids and just like me. They ceased being unfathomable mysteries. I could relate to them as people — not as case histories and diagnoses. This led to a much simpler relationship.

Not long ago, a friend saw me interacting with my daughter and commented:

"You're talking to your daughter just like she's a normal child."

I instinctively and cheekily responded:

"Yep, that's my scientifically proven method for working with *special needs* kids. They are just like the rest of us!"

To prove my point, I bought my daughter a t-shirt that says it all: "Keep calm. It's only an extra chromosome."

Recently I read that suffering comes when we try to make what is temporary, permanent. That's exactly what I was doing. I was unknowingly taking my constantly shifting thoughts and building them into fixed beliefs, judgements and expectations: what was right and what was wrong; who was winning and who was losing. I had created a fortress and turned myself into a prisoner.

The only way out, I realised, was not through thinking. It was through humility.

Once I refocussed my attention away from me, I looked anew at the attentive professionals. We all belong to the same team, I realised, a team called: *Let's do the best we can according to our thinking in the moment.*

Disagreements are natural. But I learned that if I stayed present and neutral, allowing my thinking to flow gracefully, then what had previously seemed irreconcilable and unmanageable could change. It's just the way the human experience works.

My role regarding my children has expanded. No longer am I a maternal therapist nor a micromanager. Instead, I gently steer them towards their own wisdom.

This poses its own challenges in the face of life coming at me from the outside in the form of autism, "special needs" and heart defects. But now that I understand the human experience differently, I have an underlying security, confidence and resilience. I am letting go, allowing me to experience a closeness, appreciation and unconditional love for all my children.

LITTLE PEOPLE MAKE THE BEST TEACHERS

A few years ago, as part of my preparation for the annual conference, I decided to capture on film some of the boys talking about their understanding of the Principles. I wasn't sure how the interviews would turn out, but it was my intention to project the footage onto the big screen, offering delegates an original angle: the Principles viewed through the eyes of children and teens.

The boys had experienced years — actually pretty much the vast majority of their youth — listening to me carry on about Mind, Consciousness and Thought. Whether at the dinner table, revising homework, on holiday, or while resolving conflict between them, I was always looking for an opportunity to share my understanding. Over time, each child began to develop a level of respect for the potential impact of this learning in their own lives. Like water dripping inexorably onto a rock, the boys were slowly creating their own impressions. With the upcoming conference, the time seemed right to see whether they could articulate them.

So without any preparation or prompting, we just switched on the microphone and rolled the camera. Two of the older boys went first. And then came ten-year-old Benjy's turn. As I sat opposite him and took in his two protruding front teeth jutting firmly in my direction, his sparkling but mischievous blue eyes and his constantly fidgeting hands, I wondered if I had overreached myself. But we had come this far, and I had promised him a hot chocolate from a nearby coffee shop if he acquiesced to the interview, so it was a touch late for both of us to back down now. The camera was rigged and ready. Without further delay I got things going.

February, 2013

"So, Benjy, I thought it would be really cool for people to hear how a young boy of ten is able to see how powerful thinking is, how these Principles of Mind, Consciousness and Thought work and how easy it is to get the hang of it. Do you have any recent examples when you have been swayed by your thinking?"

Normally quite shy and reticent in the presence of adults, my fourth son didn't miss a beat. "With my friends sometimes we get into fights," he began with conviction.

"Because best friends are the ones you're with the most, so that's why you get into fights. And sometimes they say something not nice about me. And I get very upset and don't want to talk to them and I'm thinking: I don't want

to be your friend anymore because you're so mean to me. And then I wonder after a few days: what am I doing? I'm being so silly because really I should just forgive them and be their friend. And it's just my thinking in the background telling me: don't be friends, don't be friends."

Benjy is absolutely clear and certain about what he is saying. It occurs to me that anybody watching this interview will assume that I have coached him. His observations are so precise that it's hard to believe the words coming out of his mouth are the spontaneous insights of a youngster who spends most of his waking hours with a football at his feet and a hand in the proverbial cookie jar.

Oblivious to the depths of his insight, Benjy ploughs ahead with his message.

"But it loses me so much. Just one silly thought can cause lots of problems. So then I decided to make friends with them and it's much better now. It's just my silly thinking; one silly thought that pops into my head can change the whole thing."

I probe a little further, asking Benjy if he can identify the origin of his higher and lower states of thinking.

"It sounds like when you calm down and let go of the angry thoughts, a lot of common sense and wisdom comes through," I say. "And I know you've spoken to me about something you and I have sometimes called more Godly thoughts, like a higher…"

"Pure thoughts," Benjy interrupts emphatically, his head nodding up and down.

"OK, pure thoughts. So can you tell me how do you know when your thoughts are purer?"

"When I'm in a bad state, I've got all these thoughts jiggling in my head," he explains.

"And then I see just one thought in my head which I know is right. It's got the right thing to it — the right... um ... the right feeling to it. And you know that's just the one you need. But you have to be in the right state to get that pure thought out of your soul. You have to calm down a bit."

Benjy pauses for the briefest of moments. "It's much smaller than all the other thoughts but if you pick it up, it can become much greater than the others and help you a lot."

And with that final, definitive statement, my son gives one last nod of his head, indicating that our interview is over. He looks at the door, already envisaging the steaming hot chocolate he has been promised. In five minutes he has shared what he knows about the priceless value of a high state of mind, the power of forgiveness, the random nature of Thought and the innate capacity of any human being to let go of their thinking if they so choose.

It's a pity that the line-up for next month's conference is already set in stone. Otherwise, I think we would have to fit him into one of the speaker slots. As it is, we'll have to make do with the video footage.

When students and clients start overcomplicating matters, they often say: "It's so hard learning about the nature of Thought".

Then I fire up the laptop and issue an invitation: "Well, let's hear it from people who see it simply." And almost without fail, watching the interview of these boys talking about their grasp of Thought settles people down, and helps them along their own journey of learning.

I'm privileged to share the Principles with a broad spectrum of people. But there is something particularly special when I contribute to my own children's psychological understanding. And, as much as I strengthen my parenting from knowledge of the Principles, my boys are living out their childhood and teenage years from that explanation as well.

At these times, it becomes perfectly clear how little people really do make the best teachers.

"It is not the power of the word or the determination of the might, but the deep and silent workings of our minds which bring the inner self and the outer self together, into harmony."

Sydney Banks

7

THE WELLNESS OF ILLNESS

PUSHING TOO HARD

Shortly before little Mikey turned two, he finally stopped cramping and crying — and started smiling and toddling. It was a huge respite when the extreme colic that had afflicted all my boys finally began to subside. The time was now right to recommit fully to my work. Naturally, I approached Shaul to let him know I was ready to return.

It soon became obvious to us both that the next step should be the opening of a Centre for Innate Health. So I began planning a schedule of programmes designed to meet the rapidly increasing demand for exposure to the Principles. We also needed to recruit and train more practitioners, build a brand, develop a website and formulate a budget — the myriad of time-consuming tasks associated with creating an organisation. But within weeks, the Innate Health Centre (IHC) supported by a tiny part-time team was up and running. Once again, I threw myself whole-heartedly into my work.

The response was overwhelming. We weren't a business or a profit-making entity, but in spite of, or perhaps because of that, our Centre experienced unprecedented growth. Numbers of attendees doubled within the first two months

— and then doubled again. Courses for beginners, parents, couples and teenagers were oversubscribed. More advanced students were looking for further development and training. Communities, schools and other organisations sought our input. Requests came in for speaking at various conferences and events, both within the UK and internationally. There was a growing thirst for our services and without any intention, I found myself at the epicentre of efforts to quench it.

Balancing the demands of both work and home re-ignited old unresolved conflicts: the dynamics of daily life were all-consuming. I didn't want to let up on anything so I just kept at it, functioning at what felt like close to supernatural levels. I was setting a cracking pace on the treadmill of my life, and though I was managing to keep up, I couldn't help but feel that something was going to give.

Secure in the belief that the psychological resilience and mental well-being I had built up over the past ten years would get me through this hectic period, I kept my concerns at bay. But I failed to recognise that my physical well-being was beginning to lag behind.

Breaking point arrived from an unexpected quarter. In late January, my father phoned me from Johannesburg with some bad news. After being in remission for almost seven years, his cancer had returned in an unusual form, raising a host of questions regarding treatment options. We quickly decided that Brian, Mikey and I would fly out to spend a few days with my parents. The older five boys would manage at home until Brian returned, while I would follow a couple of days later.

Flights booked, I continued full steam ahead with my double life of mother and Director of the Innate Health Centre. (I decided to put my third life as a Hollywood actress on hold for the moment!) Work was full-tilt; our small team of teachers could never seem to sate the daily demand. I was doing my best to keep up, but almost imperceptibly, matters were slipping out of control. From the second I woke up until I collapsed into bed at night, I was bombarded by an excessively demanding — and fulfilling — family and work schedule with no room for slack.

I was so fixated on maintaining the momentum that I hardly noticed the onset of severe headaches in the period leading up to our South African visit. But the day before we were due to fly, matters came to a head — literally. At Brian's insistence, I came home from the City early on the final day of a One Thought seminar, a Three Principles training institute of which I was a faculty member. Dragging my exhausted body and pounding head into bed, I convinced both myself and Brian that I just needed to get on that plane. Once in Johannesburg, I would relax in my parents' house, switch off from work and domestic responsibilities, and focus attention on my father — and myself.

It was a good plan, but within 24 hours of landing in South Africa, it all changed dramatically...

March, 2014

My mother and Brian hover anxiously above me. I am lying on the queen-size bed in the spare room at my parents' home, my eyes closed, an ice pack clamped to my forehead. The pain in my head is excruciating. The left side of my face is completely numb. A terrible throbbing tears through the back of my neck, pulsating through my head.

The doctor arrives to examine me. "I think you've got some kind of strange virus, like a herpes or shingles in the face," he pronounces. "That would explain the facial numbness and the migraine. Let's get you onto a course of steroids straight away. This should pass within a few days."

I nod meekly, unable to muster more than a whispered "thank you" before sinking back onto the bed. Brian hears little Mikey calling and scuttles out of the room to attend to him. My mother ushers the doctor out before rushing off to pick up the prescription.

I am left alone in agony. The doctor's confident diagnosis is reassuring, though there is still no relief from my immediate symptoms. I close my eyes and wait for its blessed arrival.

Yet I don't panic. Despite the pain, I feel a strong sense of peace and wellness. As incapacitated as I am, it is a very soulful time for me. There is a pounding noise raging inside my brain, yet a feeling of gentle quiet and calmness envelops my being.

I spend hours talking softly with my brother, Mark, whom I haven't seen in a while. We have emotional conversations full of depth and connection that have been far too infrequent over the years. While Brian and my parents fret over my physical health, I am grateful for the strength of my spiritual and mental well-being: it plays a crucial role in seeing me through this challenging time.

And it needs to, because I have never known such excruciating physical pain. Three days have passed since the doctor's visit and I am virtually unable to leave the bed. My face is still numb and my head feels as if it's been through a grinder. Fleeting moments of relief are delivered by high dosages of pain-relief meds but they're not nearly enough.

Brian and Mikey are due to fly back tomorrow as scheduled. Despite his anxiety over my condition, we feel there is no choice; Brian must get back to the other boys. I am due to follow 48 hours later.

The visit to my cancer-suffering father has turned into a surreal nightmare. And still, despite the uncertainty, I feel neither panic nor fear. My mind is peaceful, like a soft blanket wrapping me in warm comfort.

My mother makes a last minute decision to fly back to London with me. Given the original intention of the visit, this is an astounding and unexpected role reversal. She believes, and rightly so, that I am just too ill and weak to manage a twelve-hour transatlantic flight on my own. At the same time, I cannot remain in South Africa any longer. I must get back to my family and the doctors we know and trust.

I take a strong sleeping tablet plus a large dollop of the pain meds as soon as I board the plane. I hope it's enough to keep the migraines at bay, to knock me out and see me through the flight...

PSYCHOLOGICAL RESILIENCE

The day after I returned to London, I saw Dr Bal Atwal, a leading neurologist and Director of Headache Services at the Royal Free Hospital in Hampstead. Dr Atwal was troubled: why would a relatively young, fit and otherwise healthy woman experience the sudden onset of intense and debilitating migraines? He immediately ordered a battery of tests, including an MRI and bloods, searching for a definitive diagnosis. But none of the scans shed light on what was going on inside my body.

Under my neurologist's excellent care, we tried various avenues of pain relief. Six nerve injections to the back of my neck and above my left eye brought temporary respite but quickly wore off. Another dose of steroids failed to do the trick. I was still suffering intensely, forced into the narrow confines of a world of constant pain.

While Brian was doing his best to keep things together in the home — and also navigate a very busy time at work — I spent most of my days sequestered in my bedroom. My companions were a strange mix of ice packs, heat presses and a cocktail of pain relief medications that Dr Atwal had prescribed. Afflicted by chronic nausea and photophobia — extreme sensitivity to light — I resorted to lying on my bed, blinds drawn, listening quietly to some of my favourite downloaded talks on my iPad.

I was losing weight, lacked appetite and felt chronically weak. The strong, healthy and fit body of only a few short weeks back had been replaced by an imposter that I barely recognised. What followed was an extraordinary period full of strange, unexplained, physical occurrences.

Just as my excruciating migraines began to ease, their place was immediately taken by a sudden, completely unexpected paralysis of the seventh facial nerve. On waking up one morning, I was totally unable to close my left eye. When I looked in the mirror, I was shocked to discover that the entire side of my face had dropped, leaving me with an almost grotesque expression. In our lighter moments, Brian joked that I could finally get that starring role in a cheap horror movie!

Unable to find any specific cause, the doctors diagnosed by exclusion: a severe case of Bell's palsy. I was extremely sensitive to noise while exposure to light was intolerable. Any activity was impossible. Weak and exhausted, most days were spent in the still, dark bedroom. Physically, I had hit rock bottom.

Despite the physical pain, my mental health was as strong as ever, perhaps even stronger. During those long hours lying in the darkness, my body ravaged by inexplicable symptoms, I experienced a profound sense of inner well-being. I was not just at peace with what I was going through; I was learning and growing from it constantly. There were genuine flashes of insight, and of deep connection. Even in the toughest moments, when my condition threatened to get the better of me, I continued to feel a deep, underlying closeness to God and a spiritual and psychological wholeness. I was immensely gratified that everything I had learned and taught, shared and experienced over the past decade, was now bolstering my mental well-being.

Then, just as my face began to recover, I woke up one morning with binocular double vision in both eyes. Everything was in duplicate, which, as I told Brian, was not a great thing: one of him was more than enough! Dr Atwal's concern was heightened. There was no obvious medical relationship between the migraines, the facial paralysis and the double vision. So it was either an enormous coincidence that these events were happening in such close succession or something very ominous was amiss.

Despite their thoroughness and care, the doctors could not arrive at a definitive diagnosis. They tested for the obvious and the extremely rare. They searched for tumours and lesions and abscesses in the brain. They wondered about vascular diseases, rare forms of cancer and almost unheard of infections. And still they had no answer.

Flight attendants always stage a safety demonstration shortly before take-off: in the event of an emergency, fix your oxygen masks like this and inflate your life-jacket like that. Since discovering my own psychological health and resilience years back, it occurred to me that I had been observing a demonstration. But what I was facing now was no exercise. I was crash landing. The instructions were clear:

we are coming down; let's see what you've learned; let's put it into practice. This is the real thing.

All I could do was stay closely connected to my mental well-being. What was happening to my body and my brain was beyond my control. But I had faith in the deeper, intangible parts of my soul that would never show up on an MRI or in a blood test. Now, more than ever, everything I had learned over the past decade would serve me well.

CHRONIC PAIN AND PEACE OF MIND

The annual Three Principles Conference was due to take place in the middle of May. It was now a major event featuring an array of international speakers, multiple break-out groups and countless ready-made lunch packs on overflowing trestle tables. This year it had been moved to the newly built conference centre at the Allianz Park Stadium in North Hendon so as to accommodate over 600 delegates.

When we had initially planned the schedule, I was allocated one of the plenary sessions, as well as a couple of smaller workshops. But that was long before I fell ill. Since I was so weak and debilitated it was impossible to predict whether I would be able to proceed with my opening address. Apart from visits to the hospital, I had not stepped out of the house in eight weeks.

But encouraged by Shaul and Aaron's flexibility and support — they were my conference partners — we agreed to wait until the last possible minute to make the decision. There was something important I wished to share and I was determined to find the strength despite my distorted smile, my enlarged, unclosing right eye and my aversion to noise and light. So the night before, I informed them that I was going to give it a go.

My good friend and colleague, Mara Gleason, co-founder of One Thought and a wonderfully grounded and insightful teacher of the Principles, was due to speak directly after me. Knowing my extreme sensitivity to noise, Mara kindly asked the audience to refrain from clapping. There went my standing ovation! But that was the least of my concerns. I soon discovered that the problems with my vision made it impossible to see beyond the stage and identify anyone. Yet I knew Brian and three of the boys were seated in the front row, silently bestowing love and support.

So putting my fears and physical limitations aside, I leaned forward and gripped the wooden lectern with both hands. I began by giving a brief synopsis of my illness so that the audience could appreciate what I had been through during this turbulent period. Then I shifted gear…

> I have learned that all experience emanates from the intelligent creative source of the Mind. It comes neither from our circumstances nor from this vibrant physical world in which we live. It is not even influenced or triggered by it. That means that everything I have experienced by way of migraines, pain and bizarre physical symptoms have had their origin in Mind, Consciousness and Thought.

> If you regard your experience as determined by external elements, then you are limiting yourself. But if you recognise that ALL experience comes from an infinite potential to know life through Thought, then it could be anything at any time. It is limitless. For this reason, I am able to feel intense physical pain and at the same time, still have peace of mind.

> Because I strive to live by this truth, I know I can access feelings of well-being, joy, hope, peace, gratitude and love in exactly the same way I could two months ago before

all of this happened. I may be physically compromised. But spiritually, emotionally and psychologically, I am completely intact.

I ask myself: Surely I shouldn't be feeling this good when I'm going through such agony? I can't tell you how powerful that understanding has been.

By the same token, I also experience feelings of despair, panic, fear — just like many of you sitting here and just as I had before. Not more so now, but exactly the same as before. And in case you don't believe me, I want to single out one of them, because it is fascinating to see the "special effects" of Thought and Consciousness.

A few nights ago, I had a major wobble. It was 2 am. I was curled up in a ball crying because I was in so much pain. When you smack your head on the sharp corner of a cupboard, the intense agony goes away after a minute or so. But for me it doesn't; the migraine just goes on and on.

Brian, who has been great through all of this, must have been woken up by my sobbing.

"Are you suffering?" he asked.

"Yes, I am!" I cried.

Unbelievably, he turned over, went back to sleep and started to snore.

"You're fired as my nurse!" I informed him in the morning.

But I actually panicked for a couple of hours. I was convinced that I could only be in such pain if something was seriously wrong. I was booked for another MRI the next day and was certain they would discover a terminal condition, giving me six weeks to live.

Lying alone in the dark, I started to make plans. My thinking was so intricate and exact. I would ask our friends to find a wife for Brian. I would also start preparing my family for my end. First thing in the morning I would get our technical guy, Darren, to drop off a video camera and tripod. I needed to film some final messages for my boys and those I love. In the dead of night, it was completely real and I was fully immersed.

But by morning, I was inwardly very calm and my fear was gone. Later that day, the neurologist gave us the MRI results. Barely ten hours earlier I was sure the scan would show an incurable tumour or disease. Then Dr Atwal announced:

"The scan is completely fine. Your brain is normal."

Brian burst out crying — the worry had been almost unbearable. But I simply responded:

"I knew it would be."

"I didn't," the doctor said.

Afterwards, Brian remarked: "That was a pretty sobering thought, considering it was coming from your neurologist."

Yet apart from my tumultuous thoughts in the very early hours of the morning, I really did know the results would be fine. I had experienced a shift in consciousness and moved on already. Sure, this experience scared me a little, but not sufficiently to keep me from reconnecting with my psychological well-being the next day.

I've had my moments, but they've all been fleeting. They come and they go.

Which brings me to my second point: what I call "human frailty". If my cognition was working better I could probably think of a more apt term than "frailty", but it's the best I can come up with right now.

When you learn about the Principles you realise that frailty is reflective of different levels of Consciousness. As we rise in Consciousness, we acquire greater resources of love, insight, wisdom and all those beautiful human qualities that denote our true essence. When we drop in Consciousness, we become more vulnerable. We draw less on our natural resources and resort to more personal thinking. We have moved away from our true selves.

It's not a personal thing when you're not doing well. It's a human thing. Understanding the difference has been most helpful to me. I haven't judged myself these past couple of months. I have shown myself kindness, which allows me to experience whatever I need to. I simply have no expectations of how I should go through this illness.

The final reflection I'd like to share is this: the Principles have revealed for me a new depth and quality of experience. We are all searching for a better quality of feeling. We are looking for that one thing.

Einstein observed that his favourite emotion was "the mystical, mysterious feeling that is the source of all art and science". Living within the narrow limits of your thinking is constraining. When you let that go, when you detach from your thinking, you draw nearer to the truth. It feels different: you experience a place of deep learning. As you learn more about the Principles and where they are pointing us, it becomes easier and easier to touch deeper feelings.

I am humble in the face of what tomorrow will bring. Just this morning I drank from a cup without a straw for the first time. I don't know whether my migraines will come back, how my face will look, and if I should temporarily Botox my eye shut as the doctors suggest.

But what I do know, without a shadow of doubt, is had this happened to me ten years ago, it would have looked like a nightmare. I would have just wanted it to be over as quickly as possible in order to get on with my life.

The contrast with the present is like night and day. Of course I have my good moments and bad, but I'm always cushioned by feelings of well-being and peace and learning. I'm meeting a new side of me. This has been a time of healing and nurturing. And, strange as it may sound, this shift has nothing to do with me. It's simply a result of the small degree of understanding I've gained: the simple and profound truth of how the human experience works.

And that is what I wanted to come and share with all of you today.

AN EXQUISITE MIND

After three long months, I slowly began to get better. My migraines abated, my hearing started to normalise and my face finally returned to the appearance my husband had fallen in love with 20 years before. The chronic weakness and unpredictable fainting episodes passed. I was still experiencing double vision but, from a clinical perspective, the worst was over. Despite all the scans, tests and examinations we never got any closer to a medical diagnosis.

That brought mixed feelings: on the one hand, I was immensely relieved there was no sinister cause. On the other, the lack of answers left me suspended in uncertainty. Every time I received negative test results I felt a twinge of disappointment; a part of me craved a definitive explanation. But once I settled down, I was able to rest easy in the absence of any answer. I realised, paradoxically, that in uncertainty lies freedom. Deep within, I found security in the unknown, confident it was the safest place to be.

While my body recovered, my mind and my soul were immersed in its own journey. I was flooded with a deep reassurance. I felt an aliveness and closeness to God. It had been a long time since I felt so emotionally and spiritually at peace. This strange, surreal period was animated with insight, learning and meaningful connection.

Had you asked me before the onset of my illness whether it was possible to enjoy well-being and peace of mind while simultaneously living with chronic pain, my glib, off-the-cuff response would have been a resounding "Yes!" I am able to stretch an already high pain threshold to the limit, so I would have assumed I could handle it. But this assumption would have lacked authenticity.

Why? Because I had no personal, direct experience of ongoing, relentless pain. My previous encounters with pain had certain "conditions" attached that made them easier to withstand. Delivering a baby — or six — or completing a muscle-torn marathon is not comparable. That was motivated suffering with the intention of achieving certain endpoints. It was pain on my own terms and of my own choosing.

Things looked very different when I woke up on the first morning of that ill-fated visit to South Africa. This was my first encounter with pain which lacked intrinsic meaning and had no obvious or predictable conclusion.

Yet I discovered I was indeed able to access a place of love and serenity much of the time. This inner place is of another dimension and woven from a different fabric. In sharp contrast to the unforgiving, unrelenting throb of my migraine, this place felt soft and pliable, oozing goodness and hope and flow. The Principles had taught me about just such a possibility:

Thought is both the divide that creates the chasm, but it is also the bridge that builds the connection.

Irrespective of what is going on in our circumstances, we can remain connected to our spiritual essence because it lies beyond physical pain and personal thought.

June, 2014

I lie quietly on my bed this beautiful summer afternoon waiting for the boys to come home, reflecting on the entire extraordinary journey undertaken by my body and my brain. It is three months into my illness, a good five weeks after the conference speech.

As I wait for my normal vision to return, I ask myself: "Could I enjoy complete well-being even if I have double vision; even if I never discover what is wrong with me; even if I have a serious illness?"

From the understanding and learning I've gained thus far, the answer is probably "yes". But I wouldn't be surprised if it is also "no". That would merely imply I have reached the limit of my understanding. It would be the farthest I am able to stretch right now.

And yet, I do wish to stretch as far as I can — and even beyond. I no longer wish to reside in my ego, which feels so empty. There is a place within me that has a deep yearning to let go of my will, my needs, my ego.

A place I call Exquisite Mind.

In spite of the doctors' considered opinion that I was suffering from severe brain pathology, I knew it wasn't true. I just knew I would recover and be fine in the end. Even if there was something neurologically wrong, I was sure I would not continue to experience excruciating pain.

How did I know? I'm not a hopeless optimist nor was I in denial. But when these strange symptoms began, I made the decision not to superimpose my "normal" thinking onto an abnormal situation.

Usually I am content to gently and lightly attach my thinking to whatever currently engages me. But not this time. For some inexplicable reason, what I was going through felt above and beyond "normal life". So I was more humble, more curious about allowing life to reveal itself, rather than taking a stab at it myself.

What arose in my very being was a deep knowing that intuitively guided me through the four months while my brain was under mysterious "attack". This emergent knowing filled me with a deep serenity; it informed me that I was taken care of and could therefore rest in a quiet mind. If there was something to do, it would let me know.

Mind is pure love: there is nothing that prevents us reaching out and touching it but the misunderstanding that it is not possible.

It was in this space of love and tranquillity that I slowly but surely healed.

Being ill had been very challenging at times. But it was right for me. For I have never felt so well.

May, 2015

It is just over a year since the onset of my mystifying illness. I never did get a diagnosis.

Physically I am almost fully recovered. It took a long time but my normal vision has been restored. I tire more quickly than before — no more marathons for me — but I am back to a full-time schedule of work, mothering and running a busy testosterone-filled home. As always, like so many other women in a similar position, I am still figuring out how to get the balance right (as if we ever could). But at least I'm having a good time trying.

The Three Principles continue to touch more and more lives, providing the explanation, the missing link, that so many seek. Countless individuals are being affected; the momentum is astonishing.

The Innate Health Centre is thriving. Our small dedicated team is kept extremely busy trying to satisfy the growing demand for learning about how our psychological experience works. And yet, we have just begun to touch the surface.

I too want to keep learning and deepening my understanding. So I find myself again in the delightful, quaint, little-known town of La Conner, Washington, for a one-to-one "leadership intensive". It has been seven years since my last trip here. And I feel as if I have truly reconnected with my inner self once more.

When we slow down to the natural pace of life, we become more in tune with how life "is" as opposed to how we "think it is". There's a joy, freedom and stillness that comes from letting go. We are able to revisit our authentic selves. It's a feeling that is deeply connecting, comforting, moving and liberating all at the same time. By contrast, everything external to it seems irrelevant and inconsequential.

When I speed up — and I know when I do as I become excessively busy minded — my mind races and my thoughts collide. I try to accomplish myriad tasks simultaneously. My feeling state treats everything as equally important and urgent. When this happens, I am not the easiest person to be around. I become tone deaf to the beat and rhythm of life. I march to my own drum and it isn't always pretty: it's kind of like having your dad dance centre stage at your high school prom.

While in La Conner, I start running again. But instead of 45-minute gruelling bouts squeezed into an overcrowded schedule, I find myself doing something I haven't done in a long time. I run and walk and stop. I make time every few minutes to drink in the scenic beauty. I also sit and cry and smile and laugh. I am stirred by my own sparkling spirit, as radiant and alive as the blood coursing through my veins. By the end of the week, I feel more spiritually, rather than physically, exercised. I needed this time for myself, by myself.

When I started my journey of the self, I was desperate to be "the best little girl in the world". I wanted to feel special — and thought it was achievable only by being better, different and perfect. And while this particular period away from home has indeed been very special, I now appreciate that I no longer need "special" to be fulfilled and to thrive.

Slowly but surely, I have learnt to merge the ordinary and the divine into my everyday experience. The formless and the form; the oneness of life. This enables me to join every other living soul in the remarkable, beautiful game of life.

What a revelation it has been over the past ten years to discover that what makes me and all of us special is — and always has been — rooted in our sameness. What makes me ordinary makes me extraordinary. No wonder I missed it for so long. It is too simple for the intellect.

Now I know where to look when I feel something is lacking. There is only one place to find peace; only one place where all answers reside. And I truly treasure when, through its grace, Mind comes to my aid, gifting me the wisdom of its infinite wonder. I am uplifted by being connected to its energy. I am blessed to experience its perfect, powerful flow throughout my entire system.

Its beauty and mystery both energise and still me all at once. Within the stillness, I quiet down just enough to catch a glimpse of the Divine nature. This is also my nature; all of our natures.

It is an exquisite state of grace.

EPILOGUE
REVOLUTION
OF UNDERSTANDING

The world is starting to wake up to what Michael Neill calls "The Inside-out Revolution".

Since I began writing this book it has become increasingly clear to me what the Three Principles really offer: a revolution of understanding that shatters many of the assumptions we have believed to be true for centuries.

My hope is that this book has been able to reflect the beauty and purity that already exists within each one of us — with all our imperfections. It is humbling but equally awe-inspiring when we begin to discover the infinite creative power that resides within us all.

Yes, I have learnt a great deal and am immensely grateful for the change I have been gifted. But I have also learnt to be grateful for the not so perfect moments. I am (in case you missed this!) still full of imperfections, and wholly and unapologetically human. It's simply that I am now more at peace with — and far less interested in — my frailties and shortcomings. What I am deeply curious about is the part of me — the part of all of us — that is whole and perfect already.

Ten years ago, it was this potential that captured my imagination and began my journey of uncovering the common threads we universally share. It is what continues to stir my soul to this day. It is what directs me to the very core of our divine spiritual nature. It is what helps awaken me to the ocean of possibilities within each one of us. It is what gives me hope that we are always no more than a thought away from a fresh experience of life. It is what gives me faith that we are connected, supported and guided by a Mind that has infinite knowledge and wisdom.

Principles — once uncovered and understood — have a momentum of their own. Their implications and evidence are seen everywhere. This helps explain the phenomenal growth and interest in the Three Principles over the course of the last few years.

We no longer believe that the earth is flat. Similarly, an outside-in explanation of experience falls hopelessly short of sound logic and reason. It is time to move forward with a new understanding. It is time to have faith in the exquisite potential of each and every human being; to believe, as Sydney Banks did, that:

"With hope and faith as beacons, anything can happen."

It is time to learn about the nature and workings of our Exquisite Mind.

Terry Rubenstein

February, 2016

FURTHER
LEARNING OPPORTUNITIES

In order to further your learning and development, I highly recommend the books and recordings of Sydney Banks, the originator of the Three Principles. To access the full range of Sydney Banks resources, check out:

www.sydneybanks.org

There are also a number of organisations committed to spreading the Principles and furthering understanding in a variety of ways. Though not an exhaustive list, the following websites contain excellent opportunities for further learning:

Innate Health Centre

The non-profit organisation I co-founded with Shaul Rosenblatt, offering an array of courses, seminars, one-to-one intensives and sessions. Our website has an extensive media library containing a broad range of talks by myself and a host of other Principles' teachers and practitioners.

www.innatehealth.co

3P Annual Conference

The largest annual Principles conference in the world usually held over three days in May in North London. Past conferences have covered areas such as: relationships, stress, business performance, emotional well-being, clinical applications, and social care. Previous speakers have included the top practitioners in this field from around the world.

www.3pconference.org

3P Reflection Essays

This page gives you access to a multitude of essays by leading Innate Health educator Judy Sedgeman on topics including: life situations, business, leadership, education and learning.

www.three-principles.com/3p-reflections-essays

Centre for Sustainable Change

This charity has been successfully applying Principles-based Innate Health psychology to communities and schools across the USA for over 30 years.

www.centreforsustainablechange.org

One Thought

Information about practitioner training and online courses from one of the leading Three Principles training organisations.

www.onethought.com/practitioner-training

Pransky and Associates

Pransky and Associates is one of the leading American-based practices teaching the Principles. On this site you will find excellent learning resources.

www.pranskyandassociates.com

Principles for Human Development Inc.

Access to a collection of inspirational essays and insights on the Principles and related topics by Elsie Spittle, who has been teaching the Principles for over 30 years.

www.3phd.net

Supercoach

An array of inspiring videos, articles and recordings by bestselling Principles author Michael Neill and other leading Three Principles practitioners.

www.supercoach.com/introduction/what-is-the-inside-out-understanding/

Three Principles Foundation

Information about the Three Principles School founded by Chip Chipman and Elsie Spittle and based in Salt Spring Island, British Columbia.

www.threeprinciplesfoundation.org

Three Principles Global Community

In addition to the articles, podcasts and videos, there is research about the effectiveness of the Principles, plus events and practitioner listings.

www.3pgc.org

Three Principles Movies

Shows how the Three Principles approach has been successfully applied to a number of settings including homeless shelters, schools, prisons and troubled communities. The site also has interviews with leading Innate Health educators from around the world.

www.threeprinciplesmovies.com

WITH GRATITUDE

I have enormous gratitude for the overwhelming goodness and blessing that shows up in every moment of my life. More often than not, this arrives in the form of wonderful people to whom I owe so much appreciation.

Over the past ten years, I have had the deep pleasure of teaching and working with a wonderfully diverse range of clients and students. So much of what I have shared in these pages derives from the learning we have undertaken together.

I am deeply grateful for the invaluable and authentic contributions to this book of Eli, Gemma, James, Rebecca, Tamara and Toby.

Thank you to Anna, Diana, Elliot, Jon, Mord, Naomi, Kaela, Kerry, Rafaella, Ruth, Sammy, Shaina and all the others who offered their honest and extremely helpful feedback in the various stages of our writing. And to Simon Taljaard and Brian Belanger for your design skills and work on the cover.

The expert editorial contributions of Miriam Rosenberg and MJ have been immense — your time, infinite patience and great attention to detail have been invaluable.

Thank you to Steve at MX Publishing who believed in this project from the first moment we talked.

At critical junctures, certain close colleagues, friends and mentors offered crucial assistance and feedback. Without your time, suggestions and input, this book would have looked very different. Thank you Aaron, Ami, Chantal, Dicken, George, Jamie and Michael.

Michael Neill, the busiest person on the planet: I am immensely grateful for your time, invaluable advice and care. And I didn't give up on you for a reason — the Foreword perfectly encapsulates the spirit and intention of this book.

It is impossible to list all the remarkable people who have shared their understanding with me over the last decade; I trust you all know how significant your contribution has been. I have been truly privileged to learn from and teach with an extraordinary array of teachers. In particular, my heartfelt gratitude goes out to Ami Chen Mills-Naim, Barb Patterson, Dr Bill and Linda Pettit, Cathy Casey, Chaim Levine, Chip and Jan Chipman, Elsie Spittle, Gabriella Maldonado, Jenny Kennard, Judy Sedgeman, Mara Gleason, Mark Howard, Linda Pransky, Quinn Cashion and Rudi Kennard.

In a lifetime, we are privileged to be touched by certain people in a way that leaves an indelible impression. Were it not for them, my life would look very different.

Shaul Rosenblatt: I could not have been blessed to have had a wiser nor braver friend, teacher and boss. I hope we continue to work together to help change the world.

Dicken Bettinger: it is almost impossible to describe the impact you have made on me. Your gentle but firm guidance, and unwavering support and love have brought so much light into my life.

Aaron Turner: what we learned together overturned my understanding of the world in a day. The dots all joined when I met you and continue to do so.

Keith Blevens and Valda Monroe: sometimes we need a real shake up to challenge what we think we know. You have both been overly generous with your time, allowing me to see so much that was previously invisible.

George Pransky: with heartfelt generosity, you have supported both me and the Centre. Your commitment to getting this understanding out into the world has paved the way for all of us to do what we do.

Rabbi Dr Tatz: you opened my mind to an understanding of *da'as* and remain a source of inspiration and wellspring of truth to both Brian and me over twenty years later.

I am so blessed to work with an incredible group of people at the Innate Health Centre. Shoshanah — my "partner in crime", without whom this adventure would not be half as much fun. My deepest thanks for being part of this incredible vision also goes to Chana, Julian, Stacey, Toby, Yosef and the entire IHC team.

Boys: I prayed hard for you and was rewarded tenfold. There is no purer joy I could ever know than that of being your mother. You have been my greatest teachers and I am in awe of your wisdom and purity of mind and soul.

Brian: there would be no book without you. You have thrown yourself into this project like you throw yourself into life — fully and unconditionally. The boys and I have been undeservedly blessed to have you in our lives.

ABOUT THE AUTHORS

TERRY RUBENSTEIN, co-founder and Director of the London-based Innate Health Centre, is recognised as one of the world's leading Three Principles educators and practitioners. Since discovering her own psychological health after years of mental suffering, Terry has trained under and worked with many of the pioneers in this field. Over the past decade, she has taught and impacted countless people through her uplifting seminars, workshops, online talks, one-to-one sessions and popular weekly Innate Health blog.

Terry is one of a very small group of people who brought the Principles to the UK. In 2010, she created and launched the first 3PUK Conference, a three-day event featuring many of the world's most accomplished Principles speakers. It is now the largest Three Principles conference in the world.

BRIAN RUBENSTEIN is the Chief Operating Officer of a non-profit educational organisation. He has an MBA, an MA in Psychotherapy and previously worked in the financial sector in the City of London. Brian is a graduate of the One Thought Training Institute and an accredited Three Principles practitioner. This is his second book.

Terry, Brian and their six wonderful sons live in North West London, where they all apply their understanding of the Principles to navigate the ups and downs of life together.

The Innate Health Centre is a non-profit organisation providing an affordable and accessible resource for learning about the Three Principles of Innate Health. Our vibrant learning centre enables people of all ages and from all walks of life to learn about their innate mental well-being in a warm and relaxed environment.

HOW CAN WE HELP YOU?

Our team of practitioners are available for learning with you about the building blocks of psychology. We offer courses, workshops and 1-1 sessions that show how you can independently maintain a high level of functioning in all areas of your life.

WHAT MAKES OUR APPROACH UNIQUE?

We are mental health educators; not therapists or psychologists. We don't believe in teaching you about what you already know. Rather, we share a new paradigm that explains all psychological functioning. This helps you access your own insights and the solutions you are looking for.

WHAT DO WE OFFER?

A range of programmes, courses and drop-in groups covering:

- Annual 3P Conference
- Bereavement
- Marriage & Relationships
- Mental Health issues
- Parenting
- Stress
- Spiritual & Mental Well-being
- Teenagers & Schools Programme

Our extensive in-house library and shop are a fantastic learning resource. We welcome all Centre users to drop in and browse at their leisure.

FACEBOOK: fb.com/ihclondon

WEBSITE: www.innatehealth.co

EMAIL: info@innatehealth.co

PHONE: 0208 912 1216

ADDRESS: 1117 Finchley Rd, NW11 0QB

CHARITY Nº: 1117028